Dollar Collapse

By James Templeton

© 2013 James Templeton

All Rights Reserved. No part of this publication may be reproduced, stored, or transmitted in any form or by any means, including scanning, photocopying, or otherwise without prior written permission of the copyright holder.

Disclaimer and Terms of Use: This publication presents financial statistics, data, and trends from government statistics, company reports, press releases, and other investment sources. While all attempts have been made to verify information provided in this publication, the author, publisher, and their affiliated parties are not responsible in any way for damages resulting from the use of this publication, including predictions and forecasts, or the information provided or omitted herein. The author and publisher are not acting as investment advisors and do not provide individual investment advice. For professional advice specific to your situation, please consult with a financial professional.

First Printing, 2013

Printed in the United States of America

Contents

Chapter 1: How We Got Here and Where We're Going.........8
   A Brief History of Money and Credit................9
   The Birth of Credit..............................10
   The Slippery Slope to Bankruptcy.................11
      The Federal Reserve Act (Owen-Glass Act).....11
   Where Did All of the Credit Come From?...........13
      Fractional Reserve Banking...................13
   Dismantling the Value of the Dollar Domestically.............14
   Dismantling the Value of the Dollar Internationally..........17
   End of the Gold Standard and the Explosion of Credit......18
   A New Path for the Economy......................20

Chapter 2: The Abuse of the World Reserve Currency.........21
   Borrowing to Consume............................22
   U.S. Debt and the Nature of Bubbles.............24
   Isn't Congress Cleaning The Mess Up Now?........26
   Accounting Shenanigans and Unfunded Liabilities...........27
   The Magic Printing Press........................29
   Inflation Has Winners and Losers: Guess Who Loses?.......29

Chapter 3: Inflation – Theft by Any Other Name.................31
   Tools of the Trade – Reporting Inflation........33
      Substitution.................................33
      Eliminating Food and Energy..................35
      M3 Money Supply No Longer Reported...........35
   Benefits of Lowered CPI.........................35

Debt Devalued..36
Inflation Robs the Public and Creditors.............36
Inflation vs. Deflation..37
Boom Bust Deflation...38
Chapter 4: The Manufactured Economy...................40
Wages..40
Quantitative Easing and Employment................41
The Velocity of Money......................................42
Where Did all the Money Go?...........................43
Excess Reserves...43
QE 3 Infinity..45
Operation Twist to QE4....................................46
Chapter 5: Currency War...48
China Prints Money to Keep Up with the U.S..........48
China's Fabricated Demand...............................50
Chapter 6: The End of the U.S Dollar...........................52
Largest Creditors Set to Abandon U.S. Dollar..........53
China and Russia Renounce Trades in Dollars.........53
Germany and China...53
The End of the Petrodollar................................54
China Promotes the Yuan..................................54
BRICS Discuss Abandoning the Dollar..............55
Australia and China...56
What This All Means for the Dollar..................56
Chapter 7: Low Interest Rates.....................................58
How the Federal Reserve Lowers Interest Rates......59
Savers Punished...61

Lower Interest Rates Fund Government Excess..................62

Libor Scandal – Tipping Point...65

Deposit Accounts vs. Money Market Funds..66

Chapter 8: Derivatives and the Road to Ruin..........................69

    Credit Default Swaps...69

        Credit Default Obligations are not Insurance..................71

        CDO's and the Escalating Financial Crisis......................72

    Zombie Banks on Life Support..73

        Derivative Exposure..74

        Derivative Priorities...75

        Is Your Money at the Bank at Risk?................................76

        Low Interest Rates Disguise the True Risk of Bank Derivatives...78

        Bank Stocks and Mark-to-Market....................................78

        MF Global: The First and Last Warning?.......................80

Chapter 9: Bonds – Ticking Time Bombs.................................81

    Fear Factor...81

    Federal Intervention...81

    TIPS..82

    Muni – Bonds...85

        Muni-Bond Risks...86

    When Will the Bond Bubble Pop?......................................87

    Shorting the Bond Market..88

        Beware of Short and Double Short ETF's.......................88

Chapter 10: Dividend Stocks..94

    The Curious Case of Philip Morris.....................................96

        Lowly Stocks and High Yields...97

The Power of DRIPs...97
Screening Dividend Stocks......................................99
International Dividend Stocks..................................99
Better Options for Bond Investors.........................100
Recession Proof Dividend Stocks..........................101
Dividend ETF's...104

Chapter 11: The Endgame: Gold and Silver..............110
The New Gold Rush..110
China's Buying Spree..111
Nations Repatriate Gold...113
The Case Against Gold?...114
Gold vs. Warren Buffet...114
    Warren Buffet the Insider..................................116
The Case for Gold...116
Extraordinary Economic Times..............................117
Is Gold in a Bubble Already?..................................118

Chapter 12: Paper Gold and Rigged Markets............120
Physical Gold Decouples from Paper Gold............122

Chapter 13: How to Buy Gold....................................123
Physical Gold..123
    Own Physical Gold...124
    Numismatics vs. Gold Bullion............................125
    Primary Gold Coins and Denominations............126
    Spot Prices, Premiums, and Spreads................127
    Sales Tax on Coins and Precious Metals...........128
Reputable Coin Dealers..131
Storing Gold Bullion..132

Gold Bullion Bars..133
Allocated Offshore Gold Savings and Storage.....................133
   Taking Delivery..136
States Begin Accepting Gold as Currency...........................136
Leveraged Accounts...137
Paper Gold..139
   ETF's...139
Better Options – Allocated Gold Funds................................140
Gold Mining Stocks..142
   Gold Mining ETF's...145
   Resource Streaming Companies...146

Chapter 14: Covering Both Bases with Silver.........................147
Manipulated Silver Markets..148
   Using Manipulated Markets to Your Advantage.............150
Own Physical Silver..151
   Silver Coins and Denominations.......................................151
   Silver Bullion Bars...152
   Junk Silver..152
Silver Mining Stocks...153
   Senior Level Silver Stocks...153
   Mid-Level Silver Mining Stocks.......................................154
   Junior Silver Mining and Exploratory Stocks..................154
Silver Miner ETF's..154
Silver ETF's...155
Allocated Silver Funds..156

Chapter 15: Platinum...158
Platinum Demand..158

Platinum to Gold Spread....................................159
Platinum Coins and Denominations....................160
Platinum Bullion Bars.......................................160
Chapter 16: Palladium...161
Palladium Coins and Denominations....................161
Palladium Bullion Bars......................................162
Allocated Platinum and Palladium Fund................162
Chapter 17: The Mighty Nickel..................................163
Chapter 18: Housing in the Fabricated Economy......165
Housing Re-inflated..165
Why the Jobs Aren't Coming Back....................166
Low Interest Rates and Housing.......................168
Is this a Good Time to Buy a Home?...................171
Rising Mortgage Rates and Home Values..........171
Investment Properties......................................174
Better Options..175
Chapter 19: Peer Lending...176
Lending Club..176
Prosper...178
Conclusion..180
Bibliography..183

Chapter 1: How We Got Here and Where We're Going

It is well enough that people of the nation do not understand our banking and monetary system, for if they did, I believe there would be a revolution before morning.
-Henry Ford

When the economy churns along without major disruptions, much of its parts go unnoticed and undetected. Few descry the dynamics operating in the background, and the relationship between monetary management, the banking system, inflation, deflation, interest rates, and bubbles.

Oftentimes hard-working Americans sense that there is something wrong with the economy, but they cannot quite put their finger on it.

The media promulgates the myth of a particularly severe recession coming to an end in yet another business cycle, and that the green shoots of prosperity are already taking hold as we enter a new growth phase. But what this narrative betrays is that the prosperity of the past forty years was built on the greatest credit expansion that the world has ever witnessed. The prosperity was not built on the solid ground of production and savings, but on mirage of easy credit, massive leverage, and fraud. In the latter stage of this credit bonanza, credit ran amok with uncollateralized and complex debt instruments sold to the world in increasingly creative stratums of toxic instruments that circled a self-destructing economy like sewage circling the drain.

The 2008 crisis was a crack in the dam that did not lead to a full-blown collapse. Easy credit again came to the rescue from the

Federal Reserve in the form of bank bailouts to keep the credit flowing in support of the same speculative economy that led to the financial crisis in the first place.

The Federal Reserve has delayed the hurricane, but it is still on the way with even greater force and magnitude as a result of added debt. The bad news is that we have not seen the final chapter yet, but the good news is that you still have some time to prepare.

A Brief History of Money and Credit

Money is a medium of exchange for labor and production. Before money evolved as a medium of exchange, goods and services were traded directly for other goods and services, known as bartering. If a farmer grows only tomatoes and wants potatoes, for example, he would simply trade tomatoes for potatoes. Bartering offered an early version of a monetary system, but it lacked the efficiency and interchangeability required for a free market. What if the farmer wanted some land, or some cows? Buyers and sellers were in need of widely diverse and often incommensurable goods that made bartering ineffectual in many cases. Money as a medium of exchange allowed buyers and sellers to trade goods, talents, labor, and production for an interchangeable equivalent no matter how varied. The price in money therefore became a more practical, fungible, and efficient medium of exchange for human production, labor, and capital.

Commodities were used as the earliest forms of money. From grain in ancient Babylon, to animals, tea, beads, and even tally sticks in medieval England which lasted over 700 years, civilizations have searched for a medium of exchange to conduct business and trade. Aristotle described the characteristics of good money as durable, portable, and divisible, while holding intrinsic value. But many of these earliest forms of money failed the test in that the money used could corrode, expire, or become damaged or destroyed. Many commodities also lack consistency in quality.

The evolution of money finally converged around precious metals and mainly gold as money mainly because it is rare, durable, portable, malleable, and consistent. Gold passed the test of time as a *store of value*. The same amount of gold has been able to purchase the same items for thousands of years because it holds its value so well. This encouraged savings, the formation of capital, and production.

It represented a consistent monetary *unit of account* for which goods and services could be consistently and reliably valued and purchased. Finally, it served as a *medium of exchange* as a portable and equally divisible currency holding value, facilitating trade with more efficient transactions.

Merchants in ancient times traded gold for goods and services, and by medieval times they began to store them with local goldsmiths. The merchant would receive a receipt in return for gold stored in the city where he was doing business.

The Birth of Credit

As goldsmiths began storing gold for merchants and issuing receipts, they started to loan out the gold with interest. This was also done with earlier forms of money for thousands of years.

Banks stored gold and issued notes that represented the owner's gold. This allowed merchants to trade without carrying gold, which is also one of the heaviest metals on the planet. Gold could also be loaned out and paid back with interest while retaining its value, encouraging savings and capital. The bank had to be careful not to lend out more gold that was required to meet redemption requirements for its depositors. The fear that the bank could not meet gold redemption requirements was known as a *run on the bank* because depositors would try to get the gold out of the bank before the bank ran out.

There is nothing inherently wrong with expanding the supply of bank notes beyond gold reserves since the increased money supply allows lending with interest in the creation of capital for an expanding economy. It is only when loans have no backing or collateral that the system begins to falter, as we will see later.

The Slippery Slope to Bankruptcy

The Federal Reserve Act (Owen-Glass Act)

The Owen-Glass Federal Reserve Act of 1913 established the Federal Reserve Banking system. The Federal Reserve Act created the Federal Reserve Bank and gave it the power to issue Federal Reserve Notes, or U.S. dollars. The Federal Reserve banking system was originally intended to provide short-term liquidity into the banking system through short-term loans at its discount window to meet depositor demands for funds. The Federal Reserve later morphed into a government debt buying repository not merely backstopping depositor demands, but managing the entire economy.

In fact, the Fed's bond buying binge did not begin until the 1920's, injecting credit into the economy and a significant prelude to the stock market bubble and following depression, and later as a means of war finance from 1942-1945. The Federal Reserve Act was later amended in 1933 to authorize bond buying through its Federal Open Market Committee (FOMC) that oversees open market operations.

The Federal Reserve now centrally controls the money supply by purchasing or selling Treasury debt. When the Federal Reserve buys treasury debt in exchange for issuing Federal Reserve Notes, it increases the money supply. Conversely, selling Treasury debt in the market decreases the money supply by taking Federal Reserve Notes (dollars) out of circulation.

Controlling the money supply and credit is the key to understanding the truth about the U.S. economy and the U.S. dollar. If the money supply and credit can be expanded too rapidly, then it encourages Wall Street credit speculation while endangering savings and investment. Contracting the money supply can lead to widespread poverty and bankruptcies as wealth is concentrated in the hands of a few who can then buy up assets for pennies on the dollar, which is what happened to farmers during the Great Depression. Obviously controlling the money supply wields enormous power over the economy, which is why the Constitution explicitly gave this power to elected officials in Congress.

By delegating the power of monetary management to the Federal Reserve through open market operations, the Treasury Department now pays interest on the use of borrowed Federal Reserve Notes instead of Congress coining money debt and interest-free, as the Constitution gave Congress power to do. Many constitutionalists therefore argue that The Federal Reserve Act of 1913 and as amended in 1933 to both issue money outside of Congress and additionally in exchange for debt through open market operations is unconstitutional.

To prevent the Federal Reserve Bank from having too much centralized power, the Federal Reserve Act also established 12 regional Federal Reserve Banks to decentralize the banks into different regions across the United States. However, much of the power remains in Washington D.C. by way of the Board of Governors, comprised of seven members appointed by the President to oversee its operations. All nationally chartered banks are required to join the Federal Reserve System and become shareholders of its regional bank. The Federal Reserve Banking System is therefore owned by commercial banks but overseen by a publicly appointed committee.

Where Did All of the Credit Come From?

The Federal Reserve Act also stipulated that the Federal Reserve Bank must hold reserves in gold of at least 40% against the notes in circulation. This meant that the Fed must hold .40 cents in gold reserves for every $1 issued. *This effectively put strict limits on how much credit the bank could issue.*

Congress reduced the gold reserve requirement to 25% in 1945. Political instability in Europe allowed gold to flow into the U.S. and more than meet the new reserve requirements until the 1950's. As the paper currency continued to grow with limited gold reserves, Congress voted to remove the reserve requirement entirely with the passage of the Gold Reserve Requirement Elimination Act of 1968.

Before 1968 the Federal Reserve could not simply print money without a percentage of gold to back it up, so Congress chose to eliminate the reserve requirement entirely. This gave the government a favored tool of printing money and spending lavishly without regard to actual reserves held in the bank. It also freed over $10 billion in gold reserves to meet foreign demands for gold. But most importantly, it redefined the nature of money in the U.S. as money in and of itself as decreed by the U.S. government (also referred to as *fiat currency*).

Fractional Reserve Banking

When a bank receives a deposit, it can lend out that deposit and create new credit. This is called fractional reserve banking because the original reserves represent a fraction of the money loaned out. This creates new deposits that can be loaned out again.

For example a reserve requirement of 20% on an original deposit of $100 would result in $500 in total deposits, $400 of which ends up as new loans and new deposits at other banks as the process continues at each bank. A reserve requirement of 10% on a deposit of $100 would result in $1,000 in total deposits, $900 of which is new credit that banks can receive additional interest on. This growth in the money supply is known as the money multiplier, or the multiplier effect. In the above example, a reserve requirement of 10% results in a money multiplier of 10 (1000/100).

The Federal Reserve has frequently lowered the reserve requirements of banks. The Federal Reserve currently requires 10% reserve requirement for U.S. banks with more than $79.5 million in net deposits, 3% for banks with $12.4 to $79.5 million, and no reserve requirements for banks with less than $12.4 million. Additionally, the Federal Reserve requires no reserve requirements for other types of liabilities on the books of banks outside of cash deposits.[1]

Fractional reserve banking and reserve requirements affect monetary policy by creating additional credit, which creates more demand for goods and services based on the infusion of credit into the economy.

Dismantling the Value of the Dollar Domestically

---

[1] (Reserve Requirements, 2011)

Prior to the Federal Reserve Act of 1913, the U.S. dollar was redeemable for gold. In fact the $20 bill pictured below clearly stated "IN GOLD COIN: PAYABLE TO THE BEARER ON DEMAND"

The Gold Certificate Redeemable for Gold

Silver certificates were also issued from 1878 to 1964 and were redeemable for silver coins in denominations varying from $1 to $1,000, with the $1 silver certificate issued in 1928 and the $5 silver certificate pictured below issued in 1934. Silver certificates were no longer issued after 1964 and no longer redeemable for silver coins as of June 24, 1968.

The Silver Certificate Redeemable for Silver Coins issued from 1934-1964

By the 1960's the silver content of silver coins became more valuable than the face value of the coin, so more and more certificate holders redeemed silver certificates for coins and kept silver coins out of circulation. By 1968 silver certificates were no longer redeemable for increasingly rare silver coins.

The Federal Reserve Act of 1913 required newly issued Federal Reserve notes to be redeemed in gold "or any lawful money" which now included treasury notes in addition to gold and silver.

Executive Order 6102 was signed by Franklin D. Roosevelt on April 5, 1933 in response to a tightening money supply in the aftermath of the Great Depression, and made private gold ownership illegal (with the exception of collectibles, small amounts under $100 total, and gold for purposes of industry) to prevent the hoarding of gold.

The 1934 Gold Reserve Act made payment in gold illegal in contracts, and gave the government the power to adjust the dollar to gold. The next day President Roosevelt used that authority and revalued gold from $20.67 to $35 per ounce, for an immediate loss of 69% for those holding dollars. The Act also removed the word "gold" from the Federal Reserve notes. The new redemption clause simply read, "This note is legal tender for all debts, public and private, and is redeemable in lawful money at the United States Treasury, or at any Federal Reserve Bank."

In November of 1963, the redemption clause was completely eliminated, and the U.S. dollar became its own money. A Federal Reserve Note today (a U.S. dollar) simply states: "This note is legal tender for all debts, public and private."

U.S. currency became the new money, and the creation of credit was virtually limitless.

Money in the form of the Federal Reserve Note became the new legal tender per government decree regardless of the amount of gold banks held. This allowed banks to issue more loans and credit based on dollar reserves instead of gold, and allows governments to spend more regardless of actual tax revenues. The Federal Reserve creates credit by lending to the U.S. government regardless of gold reserves.

A similar example in history happened when Rome wanted to fund more wars to expand its empire and its domestic benefits (typically called "guns and butter" by economists); it simply issued coins with less and less gold. This is not unlike a bank issuing money with a smaller and smaller amount of gold or liquid reserves in place. Governments advance this type of decree because they can spend more regardless of tax revenues by funding wars, promising perks to the population, and expanding the supply of the increasingly debased currency with the added benefit of not being held accountable for the devalued currency that often plays out long after the administration's tenure.

Dismantling the Value of the Dollar Internationally

The Bretton Woods Agreement in July of 1944 established the U.S. dollar as the world reserve currency. World reserve currency meant that foreign governments and banks would hold foreign exchange reserves in U.S. dollars and also price global markets in U.S. dollars, including key markets such as oil, commodities, and gold. The agreement would fix the rate of exchange of foreign currencies to the dollar, and the dollar in turn would be tied to gold to permit international exchanges based on these fixed rates.

At the time of Bretton Woods, the U.S. was the world's largest and most important creditor nation, shipping the highest quality products in the world worldwide, with a currency backed by gold internationally at the pegged rate of $35 an ounce. Domestically, however, the gold standard ended when the Gold Reserve Act of 1934 made payment in gold illegal, and the Federal Reserve note officially became legal tender in 1963.

Finally, in August of 1971 President Nixon announced that gold was no longer redeemable internationally either. This meant that when foreign countries held excess Federal Reserve notes that they wanted to redeem in gold, the window had shut permanently.

End of the Gold Standard and the Explosion of Credit

When the U.S. dissolved the gold standard for the U.S. dollar in 1971, the expansion of credit skyrocketed to $50 trillion dollars over the next forty years. The expansion at first seemed miraculous, with new money finding its way into stocks, bonds, housing, student loans, and all manner of consumption.

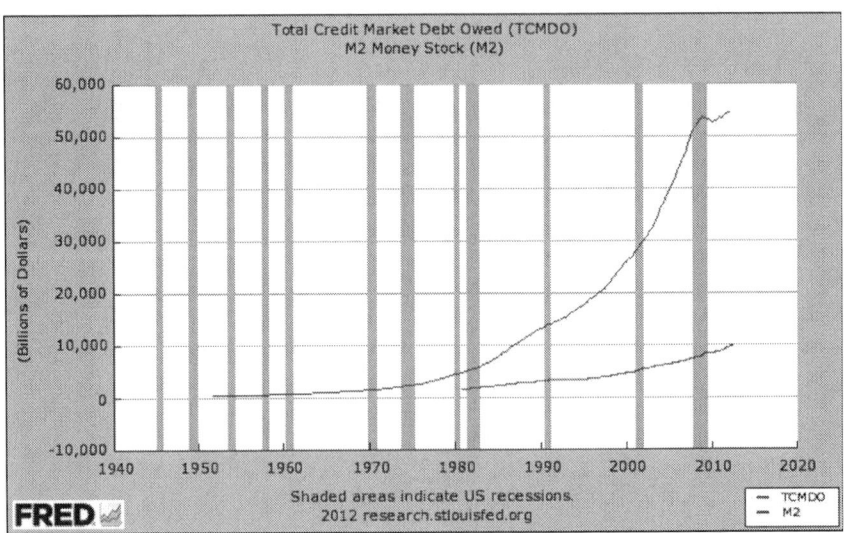

The above graph shows all credit in the United States relative to the M2 money supply. M2 is currency held by the public, bank liquidity reserves, and deposits at commercial banks.

When the Federal Reserve prints money to buy bonds from banks, it is creating additional credit based on the fractional reserve banking system where banks lend out a percentage of each deposit.

In addition to the dollar no longer being backed by the intrinsic value of gold, the banks now use the dollar printed at the Federal Reserve's discretion and deposited at banks to issue credit. Similar to bank notes not backed by anything, the credit was not based on any real assets. Credit infused into the economy distorted prices in education, housing, stocks and bonds, and allowed cheap financing for government programs both domestically and abroad, and billions exchanged hands.

Credit in the form of nothing down mortgages, adjustable-rate mortgages (ARMS), and second mortgages increased demand for housing and drove up prices. But the credit was not based on the actual value of the asset, but rather on the ample supply of credit. For example, a $500,000 mortgage on a house worth $200,000 created $300,000 in credit. The $300,000 did not represent actual wealth creation, but rather debt. But the credit flowed through the economy, increasing demand for goods, further driving up credit bubbles.

Similarly, credit infused into the stock and bond markets does not represent any real wealth from production. It simply inflates the prices of investments based on the infusion of liquidity, and assets come back to earth when the credit is no longer available.

An economy based on massive amounts of credit is simply an illusion. When the markets correct, the assets must come down to the price levels on which the assets would consolidate had the credit never been available in the first place. The bull markets in stocks over the past few decades were also due to the infusion of credit driving demand, moving into the credit card bubble, the housing bubble, and the student loan bubble approaching $1 trillion, much of it which will never be repaid.

But the biggest bubbles of all are still ahead: the bond market and the U.S. dollar that are backstopping the entire credit bubble based on massive amounts of liquidity pumped into the system, and backed by nothing.

A New Path for the Economy

Over the past forty years since the U.S. dollar was unhinged from the gold standard, the U.S. followed a very different path economically. Empowered with U.S. dollars and limitless credit accepted worldwide, the U.S. went on a credit binge of historical proportions.

The Federal Reserve could simply supply the credit for the government to increase spending, while allowing Americans to use the dollar to purchase products abroad – all based on credit.

When the U.S. consumes, but does not produce the products necessary to pay for that consumption, it goes into debt. Otherwise it would be impossible to run up such enormous trade deficits if gold backed up the currency, because foreign banks would want to redeem their excess dollars for gold.

The U.S. circumvents this self-regulating system by sending government debt in the form of treasury securities to pay for products it imports in return for favorable trading terms for those nations that accept the debt. When dollars are exported overseas, the real effects of inflation are also exported abroad as other countries are forced to absorb the excess dollars into their own economy. Instead of redeeming excess dollars for gold, our creditors buy U.S. Treasury bonds, perpetuating a trade imbalance that has morphed into an economic deformity.

Chapter 2: The Abuse of the World Reserve Currency and Debt

The U.S. earned world reserve currency status for the dollar as the world's largest creditor in 1944, with a currency backed by and redeemable in gold and a strong manufacturing base. None of those economic pillars are in place today to support the U.S. dollar.

In fact, the U.S. consumes far more than it produces, and makes up the difference with IOU's to major creditors like China, Japan, and Saudi Arabia. The U.S. has even been able to increase its spending and fund its deficits with printed money mainly because the U.S. dollar is still the world's reserve currency in spite of severing the U.S. dollar from the gold standard in 1971.

This economic rift from the gold standard has fueled an all-you-can-eat spending spree by enabling the U.S. to continually increase spending for imports, taxpayer benefits, bank bailouts, a series of wars, and insider payments.

In fact, the Federal Reserve recently passed China as the #1 holder of U.S. debt by backing its friends on Wall Street and buying up bad loans with printed money.

Treasury Securities Held by Federal Reserve and Foreign Nations[2]

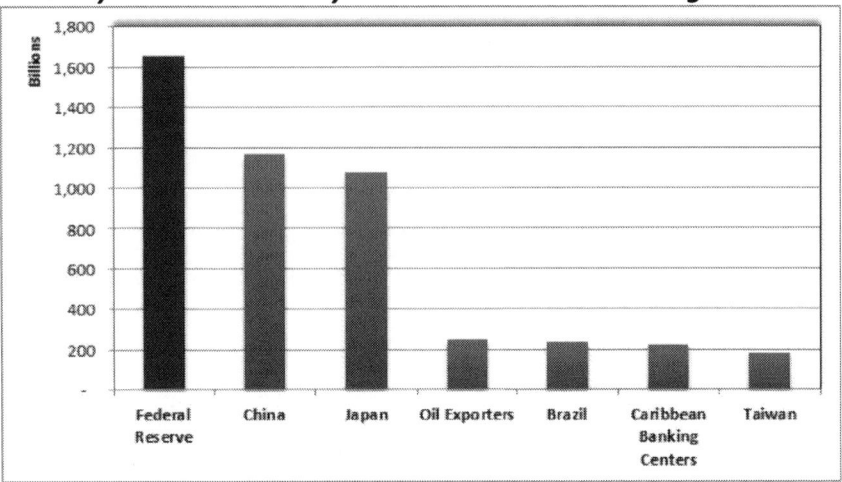

Borrowing to Consume

"We wanted flying cars, instead we got 140 characters."
Peter Thiel, founder of PayPal

The money is now gone with nothing to show for it except a debt approaching $20 trillion. Had the U.S. at least invested in industry to export products, it would have made gains to reduce and even reverse the trade imbalances. But consumption makes up over 70% of U.S. GDP (see graph below). So even GDP "growth" is mostly consumption, and not production. And to consume at this level, the U.S. is obligated to borrow.

---

[2] (Toscano, 2012)

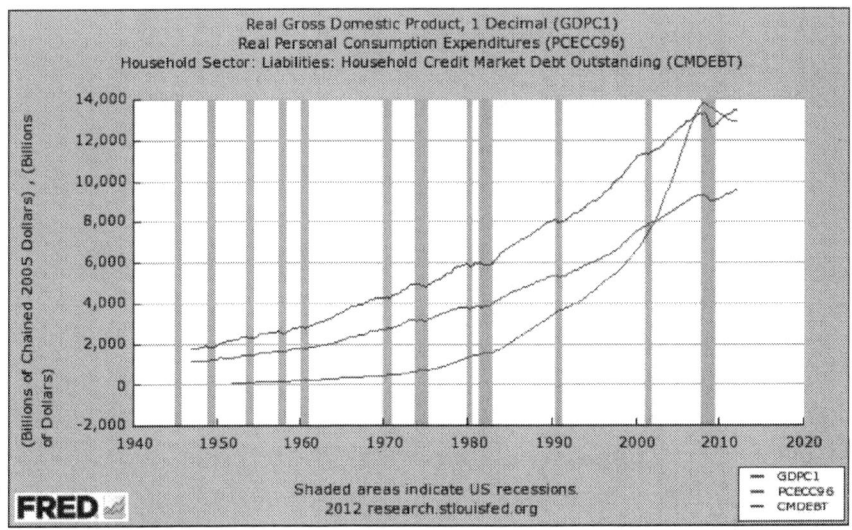

From left to right:
Total GDP, Personal Consumption Expenditures, and Household Debt.

Household debt alone surpassed total GDP in 2010, showing the true driving force of the U.S. economy: debt. In 2012 household debt represented 90% of GDP.

The financial media typically reports GDP as a measure of growth in the economy. However, as the above graph shows, it is mainly fueled by borrowed money in order to consume more products and services. Far from representing an engine of growth, GDP represents an engine of consumption and debt.

In fact, one of the U.S.'s greatest exports to China is trash created from the insatiable consumption of imports enabled by cheap credit. More industrialized nations even take the trash produced from American consumption as raw materials for industry and sell them back to the U.S. for more products to consume.[3] In return for all of their hard work producing even more products, they receive more government debt.

---

[3] (Thurber, 2012)

Now, U.S. creditors are beginning to wonder why they are still holding reserves in U.S. dollars. Why buy U.S. bonds? Currently it is to support the currency of the largest consumer base in the world: the United States.

If the U.S. currency is upheld by China, Japan, and other producing nations, they can keep shipping products to the U.S. But if all they are getting are IOU's from a country that is obviously abusing its debt, how long can this go on?

Under Bretton Woods nations would peg their currency to the U.S. dollar, which was pegged to gold. When too much money was sent overseas, these producing nations redeemed dollars for gold. This was a self-regulating system that put a check on import and export bubbles, since producing nations would have more gold to redeem, and less producing nations needed to meet redemption requirements or produce and export more goods to keep the trade in balance.

Under free floating currency, the currency of producing nations would become more expensive with increased demand for products, and the currency of less producing nations would become cheaper with less production. This self-correcting mechanism makes trade imbalances more difficult to maintain as products became more expensive for less productive countries.

The U.S. finagles this self-correcting system by sending IOU's to China under favorable trading terms, allowing an economic deformity to metastasize unabated.

U.S. Debt and the Nature of Bubbles

From 1950 to 2007, the U.S. increased its total debt from just $250 billion to nearly $9 trillion, a 36-fold increase.

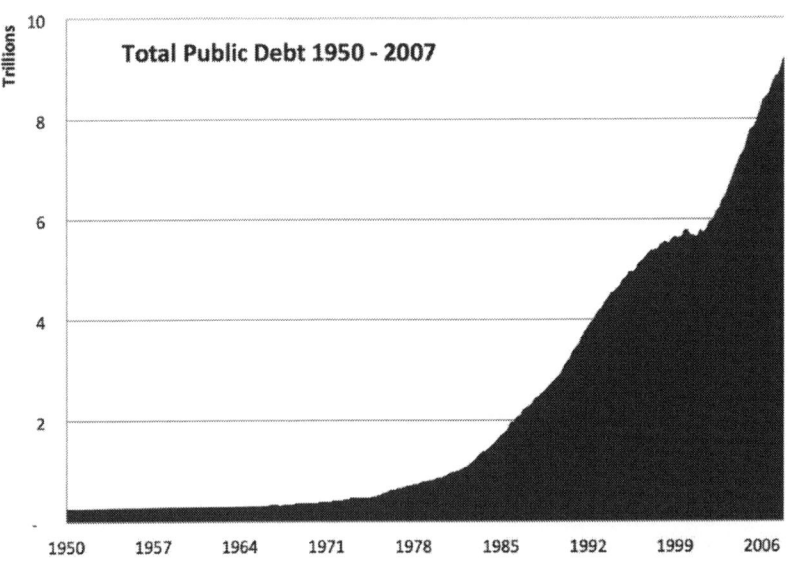

From 2007 – 2012, the U.S. debt increased again from $9 trillion to over $16 trillion, a 78% increase in just five years, and a 64-fold increase from 1950.

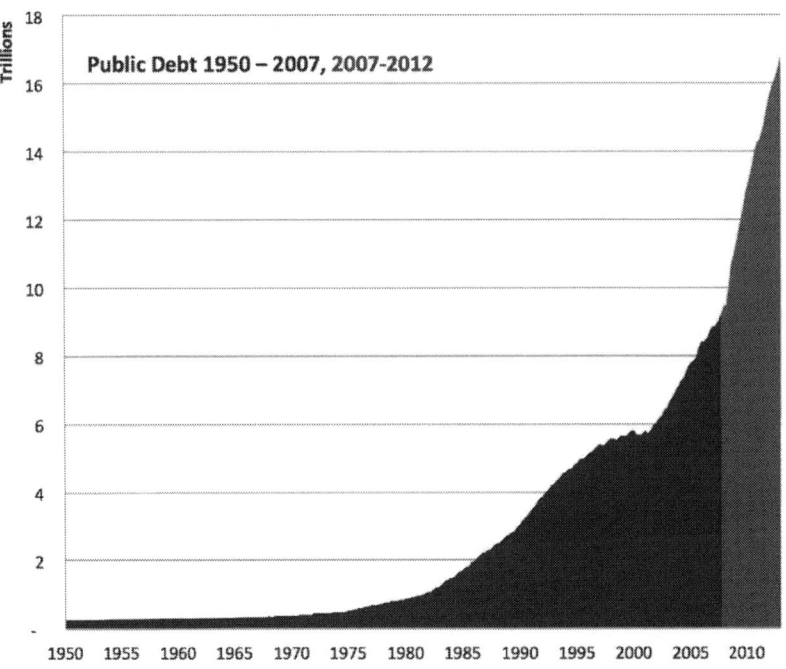

In fact, the total U.S. debt has recently passed the entire GDP at 101%. The U.S. cannot borrow its way out of debt, or consume its way to production. Eventually reality, or gravity, will take over, and the crash occurs. The economy will eventually pay that debt in the form of higher interest rates, a devalued dollar, and the popping of the bond bubble.

Isn't Congress Cleaning The Mess Up Now?

I wish it were possible to obtain a single amendment to our Constitution. I would be willing to depend on that alone for the reduction of the administration of our government to the genuine principles of its Constitution; I mean an additional article, taking from the federal government the power of borrowing.
-Thomas Jefferson

When Congress says they are going to cut spending, it is important to understand Congress's definition of cutting spending. For Congress, cutting spending has nothing to do with no longer bailing out banks and other financial insiders, no longer providing cushy contracts to insiders, or becoming "fiscally responsible." It simply means that Congress is *reducing the level of spending increases*, racking up more debt, and calling it a reduction in *future deficits*.

For example, if Congress says they are reducing the total deficit by $1 trillion dollars over a period of 10 years, what they really mean is that they will reduce *planned spending increases* over a period of 10 years by an amount of $100 billion a year, thus reducing each future yearly deficit by $100 billion dollars. Congress's interpretation of a reduction in spending is nothing more than a reduction in planned future spending increases. In late 2011, Congress and its appointed super committee could not agree to reduce spending increases.

Accounting Shenanigans and Unfunded Liabilities

But it gets even worse. The truth is that these numbers represent only a fraction of total U.S. debt. The U.S. does not report its unfunded debt for future obligations. These are amounts that the U.S. government would need to set aside today to pay for future obligations as they become due, including Social Security, Medicare, government pensions, and veterans' benefits. Even under less conservative estimates, this amount stands at $61.6 trillion, or $528,000 per household, according to *USA Today*.[4] According to the *Wall Street Journal*, actual liabilities of the federal government exceed $86 trillion, or 550% of GDP.[5] *USDebtclock.org* estimates that unfunded liabilities are approximately $120 trillion, or over $1 million per U.S. taxpayer.

---

[4] (Cauchon, 2011)
[5] (Cox & Archer, 2012)

Nor are these amounts counted in annual budget deficits. The 2012 annual budget deficit was reportedly $1.1 trillion. But the actual unpaid expenses of Medicare and Social Security alone are $7 trillion per year, which is not used to calculate the annual deficit. All of the payroll taxes that are collected for these programs are spent the same year they are collected, so there is nothing left for future obligations.

This means that the U.S. would need to collect over $8 trillion in taxes annually just to break even and balance the real budget! Put another way, if the IRS were to confiscate all of the adjusted gross income of every taxpayer and every corporation in the U.S., it would still not be enough to fund the actual U.S. deficit annually.[6] They would still need well over $1 trillion just to cover the annual growth in these liabilities. The debts reported in the news and debated by politicians are not even the real numbers. *Real figures are not reported*, which would be considered fraud for any public U.S. company required to follow Generally Accepted Accounting Principles (GAAP).

Corporations are required to account for liabilities such as pension obligations when they are incurred, meaning they need to show the amount needed to cover its future obligations, assuming a certain period of time and a return on investments. But the U.S. government makes no provisions for these enormous future financial obligations. In fact Congress routinely raids the Social Security account and stuffs it with IOU's in the form of treasury securities. The money is not even in the Trust Funds; it only represents more debt for the U.S. taxpayer.

Most companies would be bankrupt long ago. The fact is the U.S. is bankrupt and has no intention of paying off $16 trillion in debt, and does not even account for the other trillions in unfunded

---

[6] (Cox & Archer, 2012)

liabilities properly, and for which it has not provision to pay for them. If officials in Congress were honest they would announce this plainly and begin debt negotiations. But they won't, because they have something else.

The Magic Printing Press

The U.S. has the ability to fund its deficits with a magic printing press. In a particularly revealing interview on *Meet the Press*, former Fed Chairman Allen Greenspan acknowledged that the U.S. can fund its deficits with printed money.

David Gregory, moderator of *Meet the Press*, asked Chairman Greenspan if U.S. Treasury bonds were still safe to invest in light of an S&P downgrade of the U.S. credit rating. Chairman Greenspan responded that there is no issue with U.S. creditworthiness because the U.S. can always print money to pay its bills."[7]

Inflation Has Winners and Losers: Guess Who Loses?

This is like buying a U.S. bond for $100, and getting paid back with the purchasing power of $75 within ten years or so. Now that may be a good deal for the debtor (U.S.), but that is a very bad deal for the creditor (bondholders). *Since 2000 alone the dollar has already lost 25% of its value.*

That is why the printing press is a debtor's best friend, and a creditor's worst enemy.
Since 2008, the magic printing press has gone into overdrive to bailout big banks and other financial insiders.

---

[7] (Meet the Press Transcript for August 7, 2011)

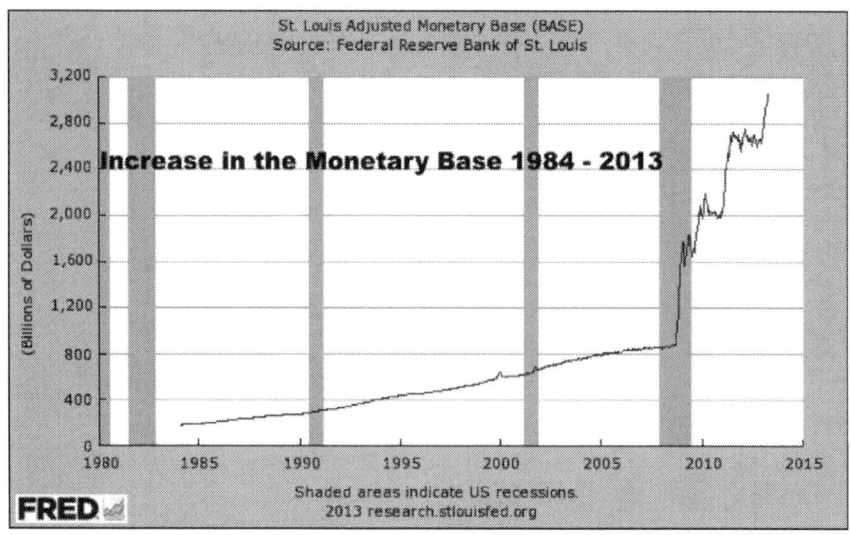

Even though Allen Greenspan says printing U.S. dollars can prevent a default on U.S. debt, U.S. creditors will catch on to the scam sooner or later, and stop buying U.S. bonds. Printing money to fund deficits is not above-board monetary policy, and no currency has ever survived this tactic. The U.S. is not exempt from this harsh historical reality.

Recall that when the Federal Reserve prints money, it is releasing additional liquidity into the banking system that in turn creates even more credit. Printing money as a whole refers to this entire credit expansion made possible by the fractional reserve banking system.

Chapter 3: Inflation – Theft by Any Other Name

"Inflation is always and everywhere a monetary phenomenon."
Milton Friedman

Unchecked expansion of the money supply always leads to the destruction of the fiat currency without exception. The U.S. dollar has already lost 96% of its value since the Federal Reserve turned on its magic printing press.

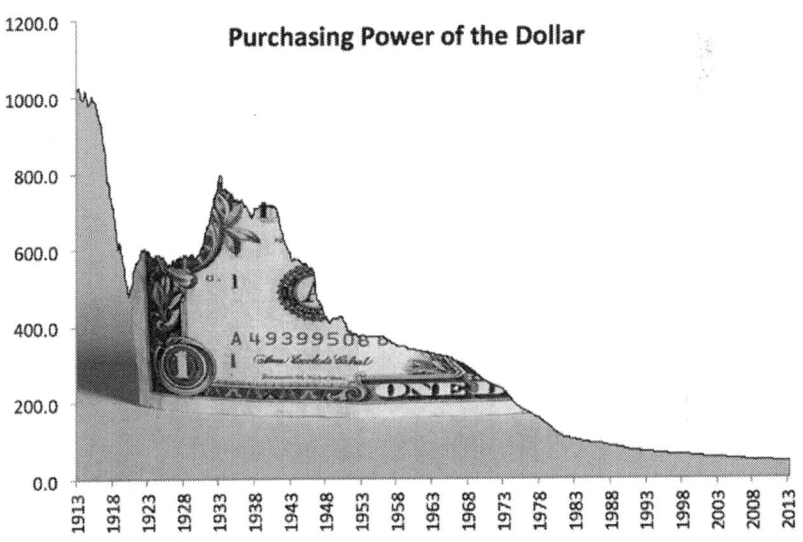

In other words, it would take $2,317.96 in 2012 dollars to purchase the same things you could have gotten for $100 in 1913. The table below summarizes the lost value of the U.S. dollar over the decades.

Year	Dollar Amt.	Equivalent 2013 Amount	Percent Lost
1913	$1.00	$23.60	96%
1920	$1.00	$11.68	91%
1930	$1.00	$13.99	93%
1940	$1.00	$16.69	94%
1950	$1.00	$9.69	90%
1960	$1.00	$7.89	87%
1970	$1.00	$6.02	83%
1980	$1.00	$2.83	65%
1990	$1.00	$1.79	44%
2000	$1.00	$1.36	26%

Put another way:

2013 Dollar	Has Same Buying Power as	in	Percent Lost
$1	$0.04	1913	96%
$1	$0.09	1920	91%
$1	$0.07	1930	93%
$1	$0.06	1940	94%
$1	$0.10	1950	90%
$1	$0.13	1960	87%
$1	$0.17	1970	83%
$1	$0.35	1980	65%
$1	$0.56	1990	44%
$1	$0.74	2000	26%

Source: Bureau of Labor Statistics

This means that $1 received in 2013 has the same buying power as only $.04 in 1913 dollars. A dollar received in 2013 is only worth $.74 in 2000 dollars. You would have had to have made a 35% return in the stock market just to break even in real terms on your investments, or received a 35% raise since 2000 just to maintain the same buying power as dollars paid in 2000.

Tools of the Trade – Reporting Inflation

There are thousands of CPI indexes available to report the inflation rates at the Bureau of Labor Statistics, from which items to include specific to your industry and geographic location.

Other departments use the index most applicable to them for their cost of living adjustments, retirement benefits, etc. For example, the Social Security Administration determines COLA (cost of living adjustments) based on CPI-W (Urban Wage Earners and Clerical Workers), and includes all items. The most widely reported CPI in the financial media is CPI-U (all urban consumers), which includes all items including food and energy that the Federal Reserve typically excludes when determining monetary policy.

But the CPI index was changed in the 1980's and again during the Clinton administration to transition from a cost of goods index (COGI) to a cost of living index (COLI). The CPI was previously measured by simply comparing a fixed basket of goods from period to period. The difference in the basket of goods was the measure of inflation and was relatively accurate with the consumer's experience.

Substitution

The U.S. began reporting CPI inflation rates by substitution during the Clinton Administration with the support of Republicans. The CPI now assumes that if the price of an item in the index rises, an alternative takes its place with a lower price. For example, if the price of steak rises, the consumer will simply substitute hamburger, and there is no inflation even though the standard of living has been substantially reduced.

John Williams of Shadowstats.com reports that if the government applied the 1990 methodology for reporting inflation, the CPI would measure yearly inflation at around 5%. If the government reported inflation based on the methodology it used in 1980, the official CPI would measure yearly inflation at approximately 9%.

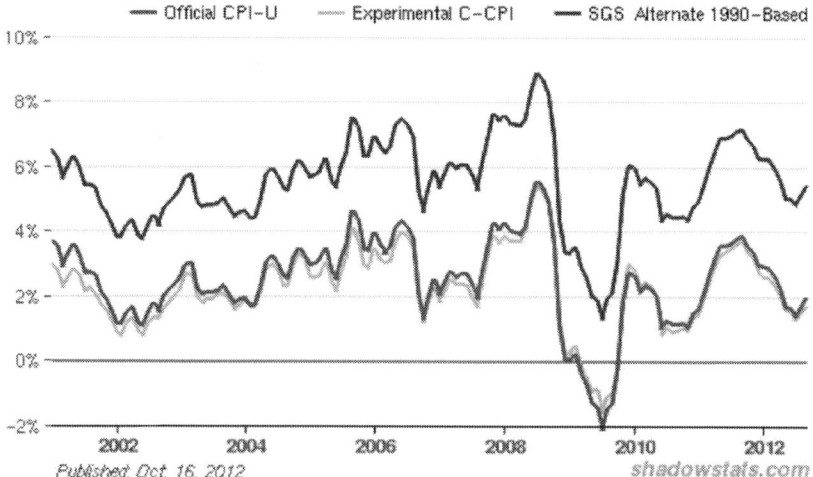

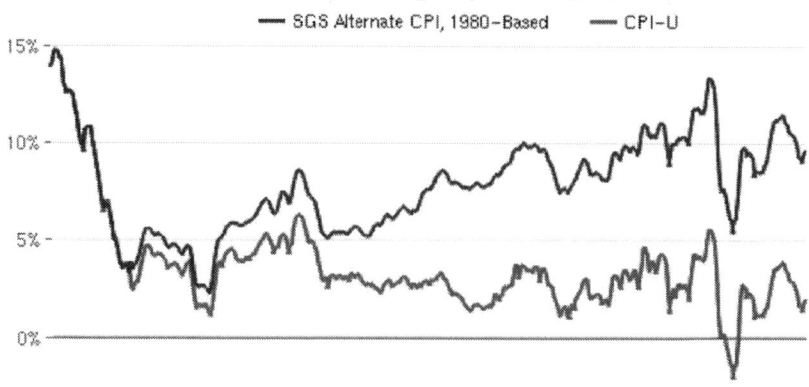

Eliminating Food and Energy

When the *Federal Reserve* reports inflation and determines monetary policy with a stated goal of 2% inflation per year, it eliminates two of the most crucial components: food and energy. They eliminate them under the argument that these components are volatile. Food and energy prices are volatile, but also make up much of the budget of the average consumer. When the prices continue to rise over time, it becomes core inflation that is not reported, but inflation nonetheless that consumers and businesses must face on a daily basis.

In fact some food, such as meat, takes a wide pool of labor and materials to bring to market, and represents a diverse array of price inputs that are reflected in the price of meat. It is also more likely to affect the consumer and many businesses on a daily basis. The Federal Reserve establishes monetary policy based on eliminating these items.

M3 Money Supply No Longer Reported

The Federal Reserve stopped reporting the M3 money supply in 2006. M3 represents the total money supply, which makes it the easiest to gauge increases and decreases in the total money supply. Not reporting M3 helps the Federal Reserve to obscure the true amount of inflation being created by monetary expansion, the clearest indicator of inflation. As Milton Friedman famously said, "Inflation is always and everywhere a monetary phenomenon."

Benefits of Lowered CPI

Many government payments are linked to the CPI, including Social Security and returns on TIPS (Treasury Inflation-Protected

Securities), which lowers the amount the government must pay for cost of living adjustments. Lowering the CPI also makes GDP growth look better since much of its increase is from price increases and not real growth or output.

Debt Devalued

Finally, reporting lower inflation numbers keeps bond holders from demanding higher interest rates for the risk incurred in getting paid back in increasingly devalued dollars. The United States simply cannot afford to pay higher interest rates, including a premium for inflation, so inflation is underreported.

Inflation Robs the Public and Creditors

All of these changes in the reporting of inflation figures mask the real inflation rate and the real effects of expanding the money supply with printed money. Making modest adjustments to cost of living adjustments and underreporting inflation defrauds the U.S. taxpayer and creditors. After all, if a consumer can no longer buy one item and must therefore substitute it for another, then her quality of life has gone down. The new substitution method of reporting inflation numbers does not reflect a lower standard of living for savers, bondholders, Social Security recipients, and pensioners whose cost of living adjustments are pegged to highly suspect CPI reports.

As inflation continues to endanger the standard of living for millions of Americans, it becomes crucial that investors prepare accordingly by first understanding that inflation numbers reported in the media are highly suspect at best and fraudulent at worst. Real inflation rates, whether reported or not, endanger your savings and your assets and will wipe out the savings of millions. Since 2008, the printing press has gone into overdrive, increasing the money supply to $4 trillion by the end of 2013, or five times 2008 levels of $800 billion. Inflation usually does not follow increases in the monetary base immediately, but make no mistake it will follow, and investors should use the lag time to their advantage and prepare accordingly.

Inflation vs. Deflation

The Federal Reserve argues that moderate inflation is good because it staves off deflation like a bad infection in the economy. Deflation is a contraction of the money supply or falling prices. The danger of deflation, they argue, is that consumers will delay purchases as prices continue to fall, so a moderate inflation rate of 2% annually is good for the economy. The 2% annual inflation goal equates to a 50% loss of purchasing power over the working life of a typical American.

Deflation can occur when production increases and becomes more efficient, resulting in lower prices, which is a sign of a healthy and growing economy. More consumers can afford more products in a productive, efficient economy. The market has shown us that consumers welcome falling prices. Certainly technology has been the best example of this, with falling prices in computers, cell phones, flat panel televisions, and various gadgets that used to cost thousands and now cost hundreds of dollars.

There is a real danger in deflation when the money supply contracts and wealth is concentrated into the hands of a few. In this case bankrupt debtors can lose assets for pennies on the dollar as prices collapse similar to what happened to farmers during the Great Depression.

Sometimes economic indicators and prices make it difficult to know whether we have inflation or deflation, or whether the unfolding financial collapse will be inflationary or deflationary. Many assets prices are dropping, so how can we have inflation?

Boom Bust Deflation

During bubbles caused from monetary management, deflation is a natural correction to the boom, where too much credit and low interest rates inflated asset prices. Allowing prices to fall corrects the excess in the markets, and reallocates resources to more productive uses. Deflation destroys bad debt as asset prices drop, making the debt on falling asset prices worthless. The Federal Reserve has stepped in to mitigate this correction by buying up bonds and mortgage-backed securities, and infusing cash into the system.

Now, even though the natural process of falling asset prices is occurring at many levels (e.g. housing, stocks, etc.), the increase in the money supply through monetizing debt (quantitative easing) backstops asset prices on banks' balance sheets. The stock market is also propped up by this additional liquidity infused into the system, sometimes referred to as a "Bernanke put." This means investors know that if the stock market falls too sharply, they can count on Bernanke to infuse the system with more liquidity, thereby lowering interest rates and propping up asset prices, mainly stocks, bonds, derivatives, and housing.

As deflationary pressures increase from the load of bad debts on artificially propped up asset prices, the Federal Reserve intervenes even more to stave off a complete collapse of asset prices. Deflation would otherwise destroy bank assets that the Federal Reserve is currently propping up with low interest rates, which is the real reason the Federal Reserve encourages inflation.

A period of deflation may settle in during this time, but it will likely be interrupted as the Federal Reserve continues to print more money while creating the greatest bubble of all: the dollar bubble. As dollars flood the market, its value will quickly devalue as the world abandons the dollar as the world reserve currency. Precious metals may also experience wild swings during this time, but as the dollar collapses the value of precious metals will increase over the long-term as they are the truest measure of the exchange value of the dollar.

Chapter 4: The Manufactured Economy

"The fallacy of the belief that countries that print their own currency are immune to sovereign crisis will be disproven in the coming months and years. Those that treat this belief as axiomatic will most likely be the biggest losers. A handful of investors and asset managers have recently discussed an emerging school of thought, which postulates that countries, as the sole manufacturer of their currency, can never become insolvent, and in this sense, governments are not dependent on credit markets to remain fiscally operational. It is precisely this line of thinking which will ultimately lead the sheep to slaughter."
- Kyle Bass, founder of Hayman Capital Management, L.P.

Central banks worldwide are fighting against market forces that are correcting the asset bubbles of housing and debt created from low interest rates. The economic realities of lower wages, higher unemployment, and too much debt have created downward pressure on asset prices.

Wages

For those still employed, median income, adjusted for inflation, have returned to 1969 levels. This is why two income families struggle just to keep up with the standard of living that one income families enjoyed in the 60's when consumer prices were much lower.

Median Household Income (1967 Dollars)
Deflated by CPI-U, (ShadowStats.com, BLS, Census Bureau)

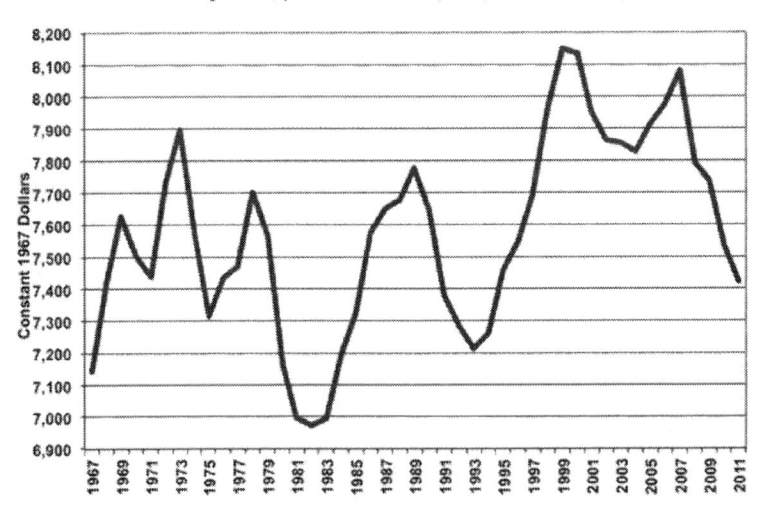

Source: Shadowstats.com

Quantitative Easing and Employment

In addition to this startling graph, employment levels per population are at the lowest levels since 1983 at 58.3%.

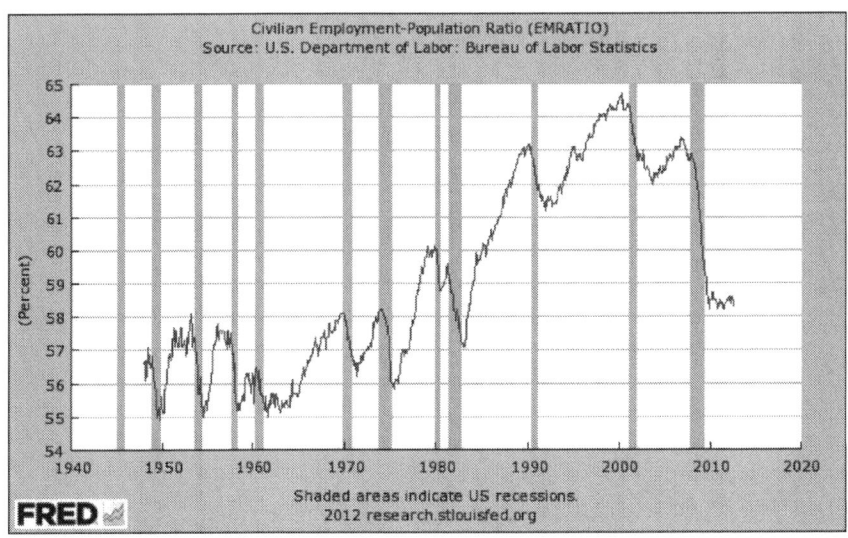

Employment Population Ratio

The U.S. does not include those leaving the work force in its main unemployment figures. That means discouraged workers who have given up looking for work are no longer included in the unemployment rate.

Additionally, companies have continued to offshore jobs overseas, including in professional fields such as finance, engineering, and information technology. Unlike prior recessions, these are jobs that are not coming back to America, and even domestic workers are commonly replaced with H-1B visa workers, leaving unemployed college graduates unable to pay off their student loans, much less with the ability to buy a home.

Market forces are lowering housing prices, eliminating credit bubbles, and reallocating resources away from the credit and finance markets that created the bubbles in the first place. This would actually help people to afford lower priced homes in the long run as wages continue to decline. This reallocation of resources would also reposition the economy away from finance and speculation into production. But central bank intervention serves to prop up the credit bubbles that are not in line with the real economy.

The Federal Reserve will not succeed in battling market forces, but it will succeed in creating inflation.

The Velocity of Money

The velocity of money refers to the frequency with which a unit of money is spent for goods and services. Velocity of money is important for measuring the rate at which the available money supply is used for purchasing goods and services. Velocity of money measures whether the stimulus is reaching the overall economy, or if it is stalling somewhere. If a lot of money is in circulation but not used for buying and selling, velocity falls.

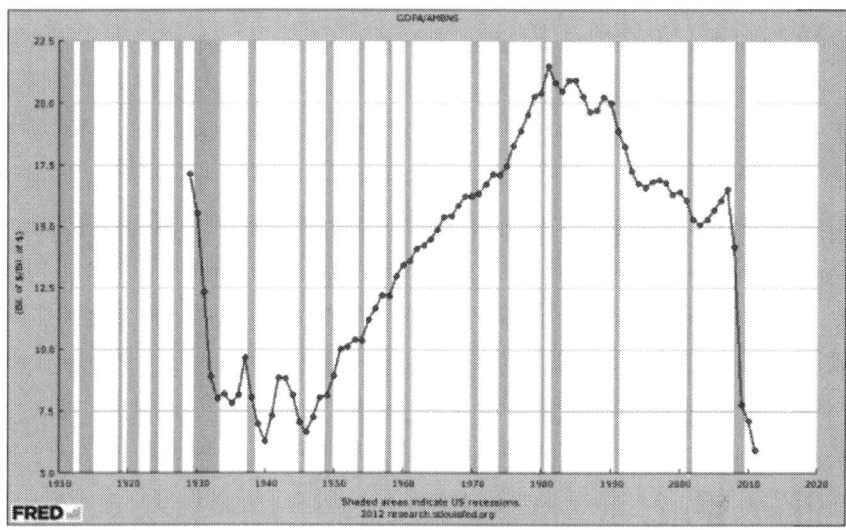

The Velocity of Money is worse now than in the Great Depression
Velocity of Money = GDP/Money Supply

In light of the financial turmoil since 2008, the velocity of money shows that consumers are still apprehensive to spend. Moreover, businesses cannot borrow funds as easily to spend money into the economy.

Where Did all the Money Go?

Excess Reserves

Excess Reserves are the amount of reserves banks are holding that are beyond what they are required to hold. These excess reserves, more than anything, stall the onset of inflation and the velocity of money because money is not circulating into the economy.

Most of the stimulus money that the Federal Reserve provides to banks is held up in excess reserves, and does not reach the overall economy. The banks are simply paid to hold the money by the

Federal Reserve. Banks can also borrow at close to zero interest rates and purchase U.S. Treasury bonds or equities. The newly printed money is not used to lend to small businesses and consumers, but to speculate in the stock market and other derivative instruments.

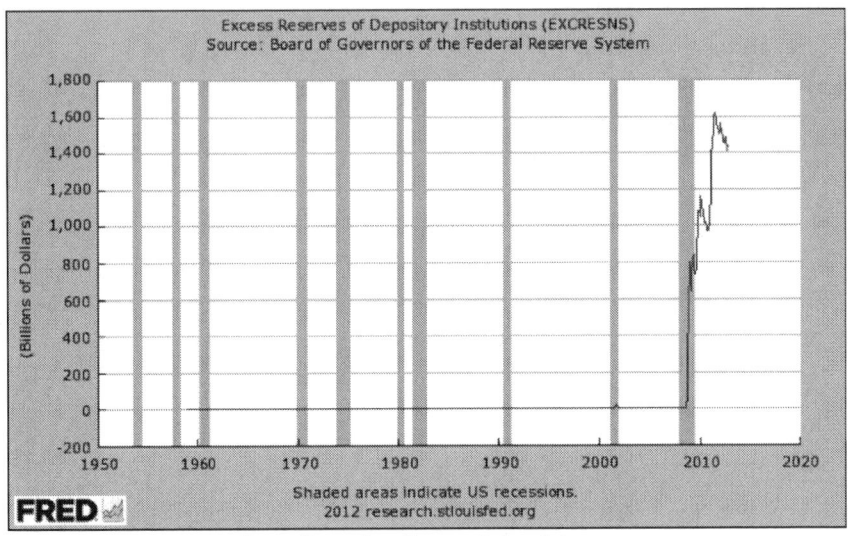

Excess Reserves spike after the financial crisis

The money supply has increased from $800 billion in 2008 to an estimated $4 trillion by the end of 2013. So why hasn't all the money printing impacted the economy yet with inflation? If the banks were lending the money out and multiplying it through fractional reserve banking and the money multiplier effect (discussed in chapter 1), the effects of inflation in the economy would occur more quickly. But instead the banks are holding all of the newly printed money in excess reserves. This increases the time lag from money printing to the onset of inflation, but it will not prevent it.

When the money finally does enter the economy and inflation begins to accelerate, the velocity of money will increase as consumers rid themselves of rapidly devaluing dollars to purchase goods. Excess reserves and the velocity of money are two key indicators to watch for the onset of inflation from the unprecedented amounts of money printing that have been going on since the financial crisis.

QE 3 Infinity

On September 13, 2012, the Federal Reserve announced that it will embark on a new round of quantitative easing, or "QE3," by purchasing $40 billion in mortgage-backed securities (MBS) per month. The Fed also promised indefinite amounts of quantitative easing to buy the bonds "if the outlook for the labor market does not improve substantially."[8] This means, unlike the launching of other QE's, this QE has *no end date*.

Without this artificial stimulus, stocks and bond prices would drop, and other assets such as housing would continue their downward spiral to correct years of artificial demand from too much credit. The Federal Reserve launched quantitative easing to boost asset prices.

As Ben Bernanke put it in his press conference to announce QE3, "The issue here is whether or not improving asset prices generally will make people more willing to spend. One of the main concerns that firms have is there is not enough demand, there's not enough people coming and demanding their products. And if people feel that their financial situation is better because their 401(k) looks better for whatever reason, their house is worth more, they are more willing to go out and spend and that's going to provide the demand that firms need in order to be willing to hire and to invest."[9]

This is the wealth illusion effect that the Federal Reserve has been promoting, as opposed to real wealth creation through

---

[8] (Chairman Bernanke's Press Conference, 2012)
[9] (Chairman Bernanke's Press Conference, 2012)

production. It is the same policy that gave us the dot.com bubble, and the housing bubble, and now the bond and dollar bubble. The Federal Reserve by their own admission wants Americans to feel better about their retirement accounts, their home values, and their general net worth so they will go out and spend more money.

It is also illusionary wealth because asset prices are increasing based on a devaluing dollar. As the historical purchasing power of the dollar showed earlier, investors would need to have gained 35% just to break even since 2000 due to the devalued dollar.

Quantitative easing mostly benefits banks because the Federal Reserve provides them with first use of the money to invest before it becomes devalued. Low interest rates also prop up bad loans on the books of banks. Essentially, quantitative easing benefits financial insiders and sends the bill in the form of devalued currency to the U.S. taxpayer.

Operation Twist to QE4

On December 12, 2012, the Federal Reserve Chairman Bernanke announced that Operation Twist would transition into QE 4 with the purchasing of mortgage-backed securities (MBS) to $85 billion per month, $40 billion from QE 3 plus an additional $45 billion per month with the implementation of QE 4.

The Fed previously embarked in a weaker program called "Operation Twist" which focused on selling short-term securities for longer-term instruments, thereby lowering long-term interest rates without printing money. Operation Twist ran from September of 2011 through December of 2012, and was subsequently replaced with the more aggressive policy of quantitative easing, or continuing to buy long-term debt with printed money.

Essentially the Federal Reserve was not able to continue selling short-term Treasury bonds for longer-term bonds while meeting its goals of lower interest rates, so it continued the policy of *printing money* to purchase long-term bonds through QE3 and QE4.

This means the Federal Reserve will effectively increase the balance sheet by over $1 trillion per year, increasing the balance sheet from approximately $2.8 trillion to almost $4 trillion by the end of 2013 with newly printed money.

The goal of QE 4 is to have the unemployment rate at 6.5% by 2015 and inflation of no more than 2.5%. Globally traded commodities would not be included in the inflation calculation, which means the printing can go on indefinitely regardless of actual rising prices.

The enormity of the expansion of the money supply is astonishing by any historical standard, but the reason it is possible is because these dollars, and inflation, are exported all over the world without having the effects fully felt at home. But all of that is about to change.

Chapter 5: Currency Wars and the Race to the Bottom

When the U.S. defaulted on its debts and the Bretton Woods agreement in 1971 by closing the gold standard, world currencies were no longer anchored to the U.S. dollar and the value of gold, but to the self-control and discipline of the monetary managers promising to maintain the value of the dollar.

The U.S. dollar receives a boost from its trading partners that accept U.S. dollars and then implement self-protective policies designed to devalue local currencies against the dollar to keep inexpensive exports flowing to the U.S. Without this protection, the U.S. dollar would rapidly devalue from decreased demand worldwide.

China Prints Money to Keep Up with the U.S.

When trading parts like China receive payment in U.S. dollars for their exports, they do not immediately sell dollars for yuan in the foreign exchange market, because this would sharply increase demand for yuan considering the enormous trade surplus. The trade deficit with China has ballooned from $84 billion in 2001 to $278 billion in 2010.[10] This simply means that China sold the U.S. more products and services than the U.S. sold to China, and China now has more dollars to show for it. Exchanging these dollars for yuan would create massive demand for the yuan, and increase its price.

To prevent these enormous amounts of trade imbalances from appreciating the yuan, the People's Bank of China prints enough

---

[10] (Scott, 2011)

yuan to purchase U.S. dollars at a fixed exchange rate. Chinese companies receive their money in yuan for the exports sold to the U.S. from the central bank, and the central bank holds onto the dollars, generally buying U.S. Treasuries instead of selling the dollar in the currency market to prevent appreciation of the yuan.

China purchased $450 billion in U.S. treasury securities from December 2009 – December 2010 alone to maintain its peg to the U.S. dollar. As of June 30, 2011, China held a total of $3.2 trillion in foreign exchange reserves, approximately 70% of which were held in U.S. dollars.[11]

This is how central banks intervene to buy U.S. dollars, and then *print the local currency* at a fixed exchange rate. This in turn increases the monetary base of U.S. trading partners as well. All of this central planning and intervening debases currencies worldwide to support the U.S. dollar, including China, Japan, and other major U.S. trading partners.

China cannot continue to export products to the U.S. without the products remaining cheap in its own currency, and in order to do that the central bank of China has to print local currency to keep up with the U.S. printing its own currency.

The currency race keeps exports competitive, but it is truly monetary mismanagement on a global scale as fiat currencies are debased worldwide for the purpose of supporting the dollar and exports to the U.S.

Certainly things would be different if the U.S. produced goods and exported them to China and other producing nations, and converted the yuan and other currencies earned from trade into dollars, which would self-regulate trade balances and the currency markets. Instead, the U.S. sends debt for products and

---

[11] (Scott, 2011)

services in exchange for favorable trading terms for those nations that accept its debt.

But now that China and other BRICS countries are signaling that they plan on trading in local currencies, demand for the U.S. dollar and U.S. Treasuries will drop, especially considering the trillions of dollars involved in these exchanges that artificially prop up the U.S. dollar.

The U.S. will come under increasing pressure to prop up its bond market as U.S. reserves decline worldwide.

China's Fabricated Demand

China has relied heavily on its export economy for growth and investments. Additionally, it has substantially increased its money supply to keep up with the declining U.S. dollar to keep its exports affordable. Additionally, the central banks intervened with a $570 billion stimulus package to fund construction projects at home to stimulate the economy, increase employment, and prevent civil unrest when exports declined dramatically in 2008 due to the financial crisis in the U.S.

Chinese banks also created their own version of sub-prime loans in order to stave off the financial ramifications of declining exports, funneling many of these loans to green energy projects and construction. Banks are now holding loans, similar to the U.S., which may never be repaid in addition to the construction bubble they created.

Millions of homes and offices across China are now unoccupied after the construction boom fueled by central bank lending because they are unaffordable to most of the population.

China has the additional problem of investing heavily in U.S. dollars, which will rapidly lose value as the financial crisis escalates.

China's credit injection by the central bank has artificially driven up asset prices just like in the U.S., except in China it may even be worse because investment in real estate and other fixed investments make up 50% of the economy compared to less than 20% in the U.S.

This means China's growth engine is largely propelled by the central bank issuing printed money and credit, not on real demand. And as the common theme in this book outlines, demand created by printing money and government intervention is artificial demand not based on real growth and production.

Chapter 6: The End of the U.S. Dollar as the World Reserve Currency

The U.S. dollar has been the world's reserve currency since July of 1944 under the Bretton Woods agreement. This prized status of world reserve currency has enabled Americans to receive an automatic discount on goods since merchants do not need to exchange dollars for foreign currencies and incur exchange fees in order to buy goods in markets overseas. This automatically lowers the cost of business and passes the savings on to U.S. consumers. Foreign traders must pay an exchange fee both to exchange their currencies into U.S. dollars to buy goods, and to exchange the profits from sales in U.S. dollars back into local currencies.

When the U.S. earned the prized status of world reserve currency shortly after WWII, it was also the world's largest creditor nation, shipping the highest quality products in the world, with a currency backed by gold. But now the U.S. is the world's largest debtor nation. Holding world reserve currency status as the largest debtor in the world is an economic anomaly, but has also empowered the U.S. to keep spending for imports, taxpayer benefits, bank bailouts, a series of wars, and insider payments simply because U.S. creditors still accept the dollar.

Largest Creditors Set to Abandon U.S. Dollar

On July 4, 2012, the China Daily reported that a free-trade agreement between Japan, South Korea, and China called for a new era of trade without the U.S. dollar. China and Japan are the U.S.'s largest creditors. When they abandon the U.S. dollar it will place tremendous downward pressure on its value.

The China Daily reported that: "Japanese politicians and prominent academics from China and Japan urged Tokyo on Tuesday to abandon its outdated foreign policy of leaning on the West and accept China as a key partner as important as the United States. The Tokyo Consensus, a joint statement issued at the end of the Beijing-Tokyo Forum, also called on both countries to expand trade and promote a free-trade agreement for China, Japan and South Korea." [12]

In addition to the fact that the U.S. cannot make good on its current $16 trillion total debt,
China knows that the U.S. has used its massive borrowing for military buildup and bases surrounding China and Russia, and these trading partners want out of the U.S. dollar as a standard of trade.

Additionally, Japan knows that China is becoming an increasingly more important trading partner than the U.S. as the trade volume in China surpasses that of the U.S.[13]

China and Russia Renounce Trades in Dollars

---

[12] (Qingfen, 2012)
[13] (Qingfen, 2012)

Similarly, in 2010 China and Russia agreed to renounce trade in U.S. dollars and to use their own currencies for bilateral trade. [14]

Germany and China Set to Abandon the U.S. Dollar in Bilateral Trade

Two of the largest and most productive economies in the world are Germany and China. The abandonment of the U.S. dollar would have serious long-term ramifications on the U.S. dollar as a world reserve currency.

But that is exactly what is happening as Germany and China conduct an increasing amount of their trade in local currencies.[15]

The End of the Petrodollar

China and the United Arab Emirates (UAE) signed a multibillion-dollar currency swap deal worth $5.5 billion to ease bilateral trading between the two countries. China is seeking to promote international trade with its local currency, including for oil, to reduce its reliance on the U.S. dollar.[16]

China is also buying oil from Iran using its local currency as U.S. sanctions make it difficult for Iran to accept payments in U.S. dollars.[17]

Additionally, in response to sanctions imposed on Iran, Iran has announced that it will accept payments in gold in addition to other currencies.

---

[14] (Xiaokun, 2010)
[15] (China, Germany Plan to Settle More Trade in Yuan, Euros, 2012)
[16] (Hall, 2012)
[17] (China Buying Oil from Iran with Yuan, 2012)

Iran has the fourth largest oil reserves of any country, so when the U.S. imposes sanctions based on U.S. dollars, other countries will likely just find another way to pay for it. In fact, Turkey's trading with Iran, a NATO ally, rose 513.2% in May of 2012 to $1.7 billion, $1.4 billion of which was gold traded for Iranian oil.[18]

It is unlikely trading oil for gold could happen without other oil-rich countries also agreeing to trade in domestic currencies in addition to gold since this offers a competitive advantage over a declining dollar. Such agreements could undermine the petrodollar as the currency of choice for the sale of petroleum to other countries.

China Promotes the Yuan as Rival International Currency to the Dollar

In addition to Japan, South Korea, the UAE, and other trading partners, China has also promoted bilateral trade in its local currency with Africa, Australia, Brazil, Chile, Hong Kong, and Turkey in order to strengthen bilateral trade without the U.S. dollar. For many of these trading partners like Australia and Brazil, China is their largest trading partner.[19]

Additionally, a "renminbi bloc" where trade with China occurs in local currencies, has formed in seven of the ten major economies in East Asia, including South Korea, Indonesia, Malaysia, Singapore, and Thailand, according to a report from the Peterson Institute for International Economics.[20]

BRICS Discuss Abandoning the Dollar

---

[18] (Guilyeva, 2012)
[19] (China and Brazil in $30bn Currency Swap Agreement, 2012)
[20] (Kessler, 2012)

Finally, Brazil, Russia, India, China, and South Africa, known as the club of emerging economies called 'BRICS,' are seeking to distance themselves from the U.S. dollar and to promote their own currencies for trade and joint investment through their own development bank. The Russian rouble now trades in Beijing, and the yuan trades on the Russian stock exchange.[21]

Mutual credits in local BRICS currencies would be managed through the development bank and would boost their status internationally.[22]

Australia and China Agree to Trade without the U.S. Dollar

Over the last weekend of March in 2013, Australia and China agreed to start making trades in direct currency exchanges without the U.S. dollar. This further reduces demand for U.S. dollars worldwide. China and Australia are major trading partners with exports and imports totaling $120 billion last year. Australia is China's fifth largest source of imports, and China accounts for almost thirty percent of all exports from Australia.[23]

What This All Means for the Dollar

With the excess supply of dollars made possible by the quadrupling in the money supply since 2008, and the reduced demand for dollars worldwide, the value of the dollar must decline.

If the Federal Reserve attempts to sell bonds to reduce the money supply, interest rates will rise and destroy the bond market. But

---

[21] (RT.com, 2012)
[22] (RT.com, 2012)
[23] (Callick, 2013)

the Federal Reserve has already announced its commitment to QE3 and QE4 with no end date even as the world abandons the U.S. dollar. This will create a boundless supply of U.S. dollars even as demand falls.

With the dollar no longer supported worldwide, the U.S. can no longer export dollars and inflation worldwide. Instead, the dollars will come back to the U.S. and bring inflation with it.
When the U.S. dollar can no longer be propped up in the exchange markets worldwide, demand will fall. When demand falls, its value must go down.

The decline of the U.S. dollar can happen rapidly as its status diminishes worldwide. Once the dollar falls, no one will want the risk of U.S. securities without *demanding higher interest rates to compensate them for the risk*.

The Federal Reserve can no longer escape this eventuality since printing money will increase the money supply and interest rates. Similarly, any attempt to buy bonds on a large scale to reduce the money supply will reduce demand for bonds and raise interest rates. The U.S. economy is trapped in a box. The only way out is through rising interest rates to destroy malinvestments and bad loans created from too much credit, and the creation of real savings and capital that only higher interest rates can provide.

Chapter 7: Low Interest Rates and the False Economy

Low interest rates in a healthy economy signal an ample supply of savings and investment available for lending, capital growth, and investment. But today low interest rates are engineered by central banks with no real funds available for capital investments. Artificially low interest rates with little to no savings available sends false signals into the economy that savings has occurred and is available for long-term investments, lowering risk and the cost of capital.

This is similar to what happened in the housing market, with low interest rates falsely signaling that there were plenty of savers entering the housing market with funds available for purchase. Instead, what was entering the housing market was plenty of credit with little savings, creating very high risks not signaled with higher interest rates.

When the Federal Reserve and the European Central bank (ECB) artificially lower interest rates to zero, savers are also denied a reward for saving, and the cost of money is free to the banks. Workers are essentially trading their creativity, labor, production, and savings with no reward, while the banks get free use of the money. Zero interest rates create no incentive to save, and in fact destroys the capital needed for investments and a growing, productive economy that market rates would attract.

When markets eventually discover that demand was not based on savings but on risky credit, the banks must be rescued with more liquidity (aka printed money) by the Federal Reserve to prop up devaluing assets, creating even more risk while lowering interest rates even further.

Liquidity and credit are again channeled to Wall Street to prop up the stock market, derivatives, and even more creative financial instruments that we have seen in the past few years such as credit default swaps, REPOS, CDO's, and mortgage-backed securities all fueled with low interest rates and cheap credit.

Similarly, consumption is not based on Americans producing goods and consuming those goods with savings, but from borrowing massive amounts of money from foreign countries that do the producing for U.S consumption. This borrowing was made possible with low interest rates.

How the Federal Reserve Lowers Interest Rates

In order for this process to work, the Federal Reserve must intervene in the bond market to purchase U.S. Treasury securities like Treasury bonds and mortgage-backed securities (MBS) from banks. The process of the Federal Reserve purchasing these assets is called Open Market Operations, which is simply the process of buying and selling government securities to expand or contract the money supply. Buying government securities increases the money supply, and selling government securities decreases the money supply. The Federal Reserve creates money electronically by transferring credits to banks and institutions in order to purchase the bonds.

The process of increasing the money supply with electronic credits to purchase bonds is called quantitative easing, often referred to as "printing money" though it is done electronically. The increased demand for bonds by the Federal Reserve purchases causes bond prices to rise, and interest rates to fall.

The bull market for bonds has been well underway since the early 1980's, but interest rates today are approaching near zero levels. Most interest rates, including the prime rate, are based on the federal fund rate that the Federal Reserve manipulates with short-term T-bill purchases, or quantitative easing.

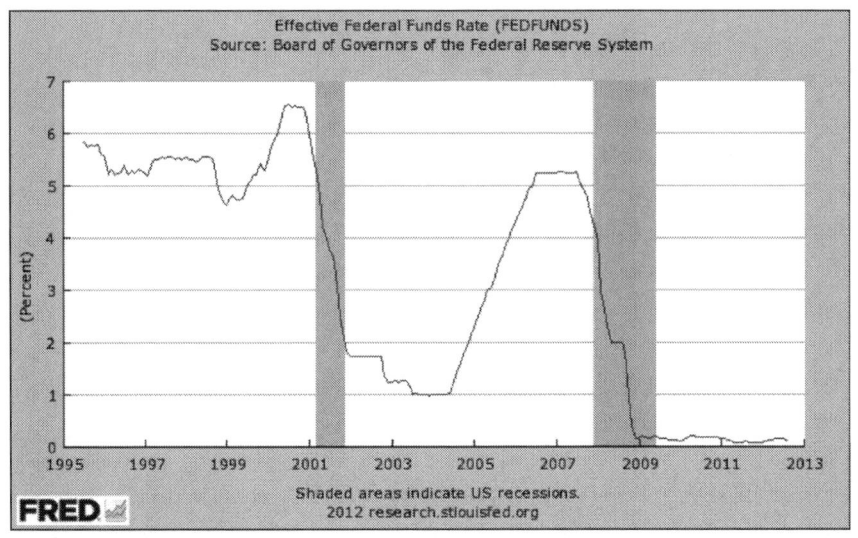

Federal Funds Rate

The Fed recently attempted a less aggressive program called "Operation Twist" which focused on selling short-term securities for longer-term instruments, thereby lowering long-term interest rates without printing money. Operation Twist was subsequently replaced with the more aggressive policy of quantitative easing, or continuing to buy long-term debt with printed money.

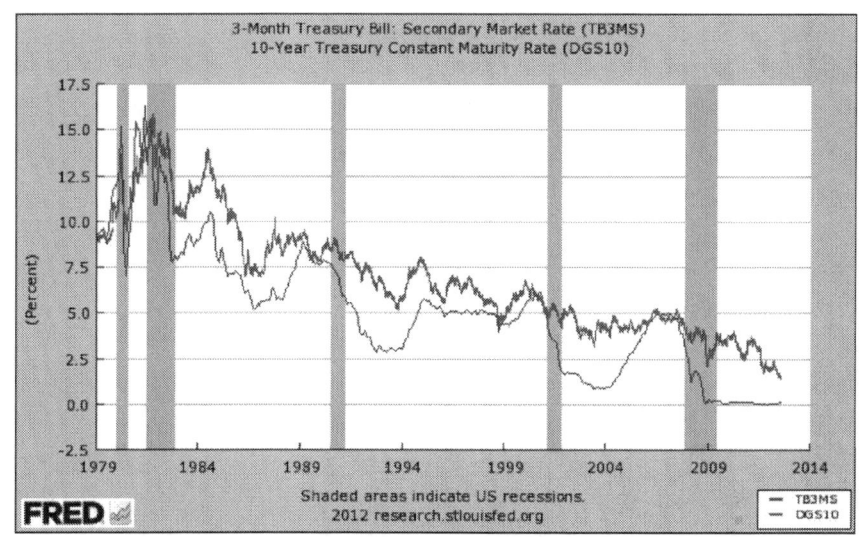

The Federal Reserve has stated its intention to keep short-term interest rates at zero through 2015, while also attempting to lower long-term interest rates (top line) through continuing the policy of Quantitative Easing.

Savers Punished

Artificially low interest rates destroy capital investments because savers are no longer rewarded for saving. In fact, they are seeing their savings destroyed with the debasement of the U.S. dollar. It is better to spend a dollar today than to save it at negative returns. Even if you took a paltry CD at an annual rate of 1%, inflation would not only wipe out the return but the value of the savings itself. This is especially damaging to senior citizens who rely on fixed income and who worked their whole lives to accumulate savings, only to see it eaten away by negative real returns (inflation rates less CD rates).

Even a ten year treasury note yields less than 2%, which is less than the highly suspect CPI inflation index of 2%, for a real negative return on these "safe" investments.

Bond vigilantes traditionally corrected these lopsided policies by dumping bonds to increase interest rates in protest of such a distorted, upside down economy. Now the central banks simply intervene and buy bonds. This means the bond market is now also a bubble based on *artificial demand created by central banks*. Even if bond vigilantes dump bonds to raise interest rates, the Federal Reserve is there to scoop them up with more printed money.

This provides money to the banks for massive gambles, backed by the full faith and credit of the American taxpayer. The scheme transfers wealth from the middle class to the wealthy because low interest rates take money from savers to provide borrowers and speculators with first use of the money at low cost, and then passes the devalued currency to the taxpayer over time. *The losses can be measured by what the interest rate should have been in a free market vs. what the Federal Reserve sets it at, in addition to increased inflation, which conservatively amounts to hundreds of billions of dollars a year in lost savings.*

What is so disingenuous about proposed austerity measures is that Americans have already paid billions in lost revenue from low interest rates, and have already bailed out the banks.

Lower Interest Rates Fund Government Excess

The other main reason for quantitative easing in addition to propping up bank assets is that it allows the government to continue to fund its deficit spending at much lower costs. The Federal Reserve can buy bonds indefinitely and fund the government while keeping interest rates artificially low. The longer the Fed can keep interest rates low, the longer the U.S. government can borrow with substantially reduced interest expenses.

Debt ——Interest

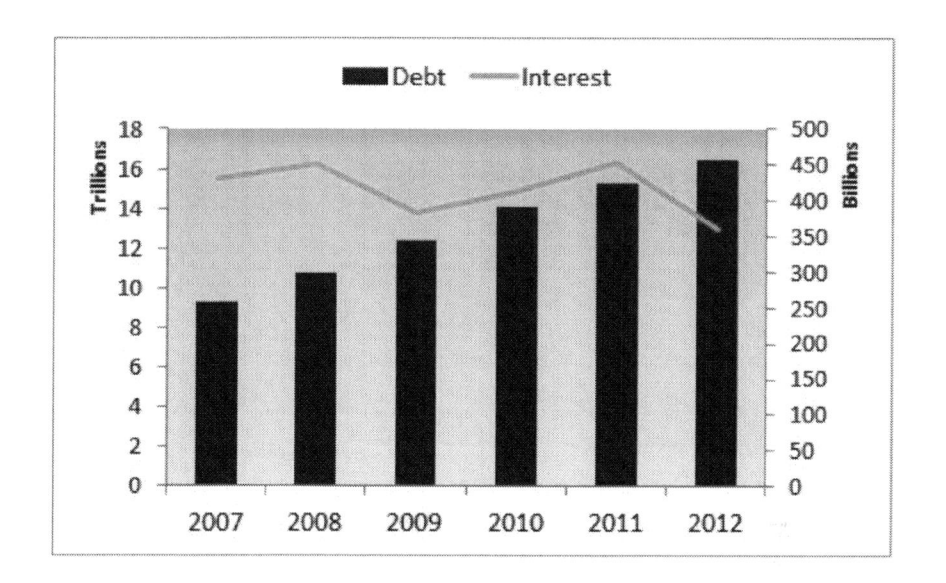

For example, even though U.S. debt increased from $9 trillion to over $16 trillion from 2007 to 2012, interest payments actually decreased from $430 billion in 2007 to approximately $360 billion in 2012.[24] How is that possible? The Federal Reserve has lowered its benchmark rate of interest from 5.02% in August of 2007 to nearly 0% over the past several years.

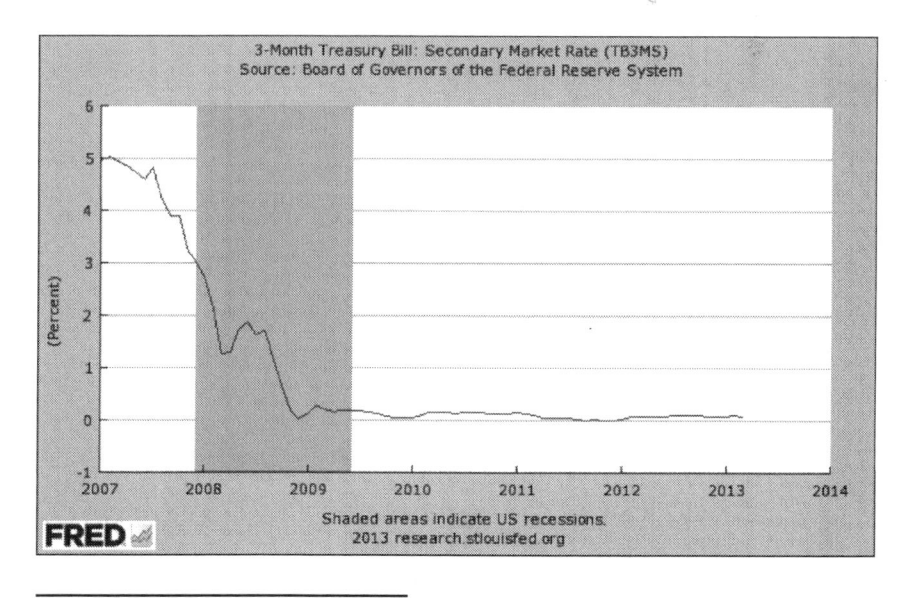

---

[24] (Government - Interest Expense on the Outstanding Debt, 2013)

The U.S. Treasury paid an average of only .02% on the ninety day Treasury Bill in 2012, and .17% on a one year Treasury Bill. That is how the government can pay such low interest costs on such enormous amounts of debt.

However, if other countries drop the U.S. dollar, the Federal Reserve will not be able to funds the deficit with printed money. It can only trade printed U.S. dollars for debt, and if the dollars are not absorbed worldwide, the excess supply of dollars combined with falling demand will lead to a rapidly devaluing dollar. The U.S. dollar and the bond markets therefore represent the final bubble to burst from this artificial stimulus.

Most investors buying U.S. Treasury bonds and betting on lower interest rates have no intention of holding the bonds to maturity and losing money in real returns. Instead, they simply buy bonds with promises from the Federal Reserve to purchase more bonds (when interest rates go down, bond prices go up), and sell the bonds for capital gains as interest rates head lower. The U.S. bond market is reaching the point where interest rates cannot go much lower, and like a game of musical chairs, those left holding the bonds when interest rates begin to rise will be stuck with mounting losses.

The U.S. government cannot pay back its debt, and will even have a hard time with the interest.

With interest rates at less than 2%, federal debt service payments are $300 billion per year. If the interest rate were to rise to just 5%, then the federal government's debt service payments would skyrocket to $800 billion, or over 30% of total tax revenues. This is assuming the debt remains stable, which it most surely will not. Debt service payments on rising interest rates with rising debt are more likely to exceed 40% of total tax revenues.

That is why Fed is desperate to keep interest rates low. Once they begin to rise, the financial disruptions we experienced in 2008 will look like a spring shower compared to the financial storm brewing right now with gathering force.

Libor Scandal – Tipping Point

The London Interbank Offered Rate (LIBOR) is the international bedrock rate at which banks around the world borrow funds, but it is also increasingly important for U.S. loans as well. In fact, the Federal Reserve Bank of Cleveland reported that nearly all sub-prime mortgages in Ohio were tied to Libor by 2007 and half of prime mortgages by 2008.[25]

The Libor rate is also the rate on which over $800 trillion in derivatives rests. Artificially lowering this interest rate allows banks to appear to stay solvent when in fact their loans on the books are worth much less. Higher interest rates would reflect a lower value of loans. Recently it was discovered that from 2005-2012 Libor rates were rigged to directly profit from trades and to make the banks appear healthier than they actually were. This is the thread from which our fragile financial system was sewn in fraud.

---

[25] (Schweitzer, 2009)

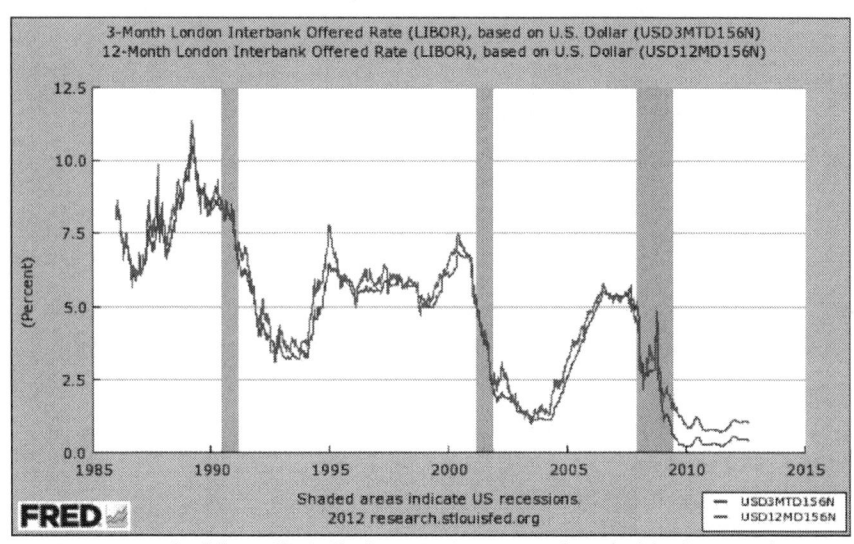

LIBOR Rates held artificially low to improve banks' balance sheets

Though banks like Barclays involved in the fraud were fined only miniscule amounts compared to total assets, the coming market corrections may not be so merciful. Many banks have held highly risky assets based on fraudulently low interest rates for years, adding even more risk. When investors factor in the actual risk of assets held by banks, many banks will collapse from the rising interest rates.

Savings, Checking, CD's, and Deposit Accounts vs. Money Market Funds

It is important to distinguish between savings, checking accounts, certificates of deposit (CDs) and money market deposit accounts that are all insured by the FDIC up to the legal limit of $250,000. *Money market deposit accounts* earn interest at an amount determined by the financial institution where your funds are deposited.

Money market funds that invest in mutual funds, treasury securities, corporate bonds, or other investment vehicles are not insured by the FDIC. For safe and highly liquid accounts, simply opt for a higher yield checking account backed by the FDIC. Not only do money market funds offer paltry returns, but investors risk losing funds due to bank failures in accounts not insured by the FDIC.

In an era of teetering financial institutions, "missing" funds, and overall financial dishonesty, there is no reason to have a low interest money market fund not backed by the FDIC over a money market deposit account or checking account with similar yields.

Money Market Fund Yields: Not Worth the Risk

Symbol	Money Market Fund	7 day	1 Yr	3 Yr	5 Yr	10 Yr
SWAXX	Schwab Value Advantage	0.10%	0.03%	0.07%	.90%	1.91%
VMMXX	Vanguard Prime	.04%	.06%	.06%	.91%	1.87%
FRTXX	Fidelity Retirement	.01%	.01%	.02%	.94%	1.86%
SPRXX	Fidelity Money Market	.01%	.01%	.03%	.94%	1.85%

Source: Morningstar

With the Federal Reserve keeping interest rates low, money is moving out of Money Market Funds with abysmal returns, where even three month Treasury Bills yielding .1% offer better returns. This is another way the Federal Reserve finances the federal government by siphoning off funds from other accounts towards treasuries to keep demand higher and interest rates as low as possible.

As we will see, this does not make U. S. Treasury Securities a safe haven for your money, but rather ticking time bombs ready to explode.

Chapter 8: Derivatives and the Road to Ruin

Credit Default Swaps

JP Morgan invented credit derivatives in the 1990's. A credit default swap (CDS) is an agreement between the seller and the buyer, each called a "counterparty" to the contract, in which the seller of the CDS will compensate the buyer in the event of a loan default. In return the buyer of the credit default swap makes a series of payments, called the spread or the fee, to the seller of the credit default swap in exchange for a payoff in the event the loan defaults.

For example a 30-basis point spread (.3%) on a $10 million contract would result in the buyer paying $30,000 a year for the credit default swap. The spread in basis point depends on the amount of risk that the asset will eventually default during the contract period.

In addition to shedding the risk by taking on credit derivatives, banks can write credit default swaps on bundles of loans and sell them based on risk levels. Investors could choose which risk level they wanted to take. The higher the risk that the underlying asset will default, the higher the spread or fees that the buyer must pay for the contract.

In the event of a default, the buyer receives compensation based on the loan amount defaulted on (the credit default portion of the CDS), and the seller gets to take possession to any remaining salvage value of the bond (the swap portion of the CDS). Thus the name credit default swap.

Credit derivatives allow banks to skirt capital requirements by offloading its risk for loans, similar to taking out insurance.

Because the bank has essentially insured its loans, capital is freed up to make even more loans. This allows banks to take on virtually unlimited amounts of debt. (Lenders also are not required to account for loans backed by Fannie Mae and Freddie Mac for the same reason since in this case the government guarantees them).

Most credit default swaps are in the $10-$20 million range, and are for one to ten years with the average contract written for about five years. The holder of a bond, for example, may buy protection against the default of the bond, similar to credit insurance. This is called a hedge because the counterparty to the contract owns the asset, in this case the bond, and is hedging against a possible default on the bond.

Soon, however, banks wrote synthetic or naked credit default swaps, which were credit default agreements on loans that the bank did not even own. Credit could be bought and sold on the same assets over and over again by different counterparties. Counterparties merely speculating on the performance of an asset created their own leveraged debt obligations. Because the transactions were private, the banks could easily hide the risk.

Unlike insurance, banks and insurers like AIG did not actually have to show that they had money for a claim. In essence, synthetic collateralized debt obligations (CDO's) were unregulated and off the balance sheet of banks. Later, these CDO's would be offered for sub-prime mortgages, many fraudulently rated triple AAA by the credit rating agencies. Naked CDO's constitute most of the CDO's on the market today.

As discussed in Chapter 1, through the magic of fractional reserve banking banks do not actually have the money on hand for all claims on deposits. In fact, most of it is loaned out. A run on the bank always exposes this precarious situation.

Similarly, a run on CDS's or CDO's, as was experienced in the financial crisis of 2008, showed that companies did not have the capital to cover the contracts they wrote. It is similar to an insurance company that did not have the money to pay a homeowner on a fire insurance policy whose house had burned down. In this case, the insurance was not regulated, and the fire was the sub-prime mortgage crisis that spread to the wider mortgage and credit markets.

In the case of a synthetic collateralized debt obligation, parties simply bet that someone else's house would burn down. For example, investors purchased CDO's essentially betting that Lehman Brothers would go bankrupt under the pressure of bad mortgages that it held on its books. When AIG took this "bet," in return for the millions in fees that it generated from selling the contract, it was inconceivable that Lehman would actually go bankrupt. Of course this is exactly what happened, and AIG was left holding billions in CDO contracts for which it did not have the capital to pay.

Credit Default Obligations are not Insurance

With insurance you must own the asset to insure it, and terminating the insurance is simply a matter of no longer paying the premium. Because the buyer of a synthetic CDO does not own the underlying asset, the buyer of the synthetic CDO is no longer hedging but merely speculating that the asset will go into default. Insurance companies must also show that they have loss reserves available to pay the claim on the insured asset. Because CDO's are not regulated, there is no requirement to show that the banks or financial institutions writing them have the capital required to pay the contract. Insurance must also disclose all risks, while CDO's do not need to disclose the many risks associated with the product.

CDO's and the Escalating Financial Crisis

The relationship between CDO's and the financial crisis can be traced to both the repeal of Glass – Steagall Act in 1999, where the firewall between commercial banks and securities activity was removed, and the low interest rate policy of the Federal Reserve.

Banks traditionally held loans to maturity, so lending requirements were much stricter resulting in loans of higher quality. It was in the bank's best interest to seek high quality borrowers to maximize returns and minimize bad debts and defaults since loans were held on the books for years and even decades.

Securitization allowed banks to sell loans worldwide, thus reducing lending standards since banks no longer held the loans on their own balance sheet until maturity. Securitization also provided a profitable source of loan fees and bonuses based on loan volume instead of loan quality.

The Federal Reserve fueled the securitization mania by keeping interest rates low. The Federal Reserve lowered the Federal Funds rate from 6.5% in 2000 to 1% in 2003.[26]

From 1997-2006 housing prices increased 125%.[27] Banks made hefty fees for securitizing these mortgages. In order to get more mortgages for securitization, mortgage lenders lowered their underwriting standards to write riskier loans to less credit worthy borrowers.

Rating agencies also made hefty fees through securitization by churning out toxic loans with gold plated ratings.

---

[26] (Federal Reserve Bank, 2013)
[27] (Federal Reserve Bank, 2012)

The demand for more mortgages to sell to the world through securitization was insatiable. Working from good credit to bad, banks wrote riskier and risker loans, and offloaded the risk to counterparties by purchasing CDS's. Commercial banks and trust companies increased CDS contracts by almost tenfold from 1998-2008.[28] [29] Financial institutions became highly leveraged with CDS without the capacity to pay them off. Even a small percentage of defaults in the CDS market would wipe out the biggest banks on Wall Street holding these highly leveraged financial positions.

Zombie Banks on Life Support

Most banks are still on the life support of low interest rates to keep this economic charade going. For example, 77% of net revenue at JP Morgan was due to federal subsidies in the form of low interest rates.[30]

In addition to this, the top 25 banks hold derivative instruments totaling $250 trillion that are tied from everything to the European Banking Sector to junk bonds. Banks are taking on this massive risk with additional liquidity provided by the Fed for sheer speculation with the backing of U.S. taxpayers.

For example, five of the largest banks are exposed to 96% of the $250 trillion in gross notional amount of derivative contracts outstanding at the top 25 commercial banks.[31]

---

[28] (OCC, OCC Bank Derivatives Report Fourth Quarter 1998, 1998)
[29] (OCC, OCC's Quarterly Report on Bank Trading and Derivatives Activities Fourth Quarter 2008, 2008)
[30] (Bloomberg, 2012)
[31] (OCC, OCC's Quarterly Report on Bank Trading and Derivatives Activities Fourth Quarter 2012, 2012)

Total Derivatives and Assets of Biggest Banks

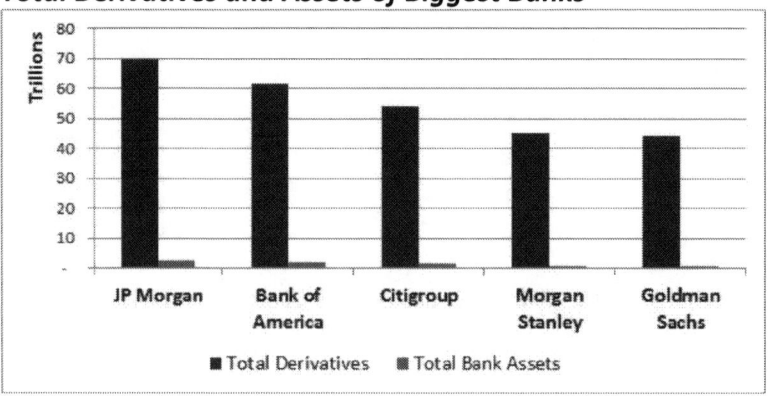

Derivative Exposure

Banks argue that these are notional amounts of the derivatives that do not represent the amount of cash at risk. An interest rate swap on a $10 million derivative, for example, has a cash risk equal to changes in the interest rate. If interest rates move the wrong way by 1% on $10 million derivative contract, for example, there is a 1% risk or a one hundred thousand dollars cash risk, not the entire notional amount of $10 million.

Other notional amounts are in fact at risk, including bonds and loans for which the seller of a derivative must pay the full amount of the default, such as a credit default swaps. Though only a small percentage of the total notional amount of the derivatives market represents total cash risk, even a small percentage of a $250 trillion market for just the top 25 U.S. banks alone is more than most national GDP's.

In fact, Goldman Sachs and JP Morgan, two of the largest purveyors of credit default instruments, insure against entire nations defaulting on sovereign bonds. How can an investment firm insure against an entire nation going bankrupt? Goldman Sachs and JP Morgan install their proxies in the form of lobbyists and employees all over the world in key regulatory positions, central banks, and governments for two main reasons:

1). to encourage regulatory officials to never declare a default on the bonds, thereby preventing JP Morgan and Goldman Sachs from having to pay out on credit default swaps.
2). to encourage central banks and governments to provide bank bailouts to the banks at the taxpayers' expense when bets go wrong.

For example, in 2012 when Greece restructured its debt with a 53.5% haircut to creditors, the International Swaps and Derivatives Association (ISDA) stated that the haircut did not constitute a "credit event" since there remained some salvage value in the bonds. But the very nature of a credit default swap is to hand the salvage value of the bond to the seller in the event of a default. Nonetheless a 54% haircut did not trigger a payout of the CDS's. The ISDA was standing in the way of calculated risk to protect Goldman Sachs.

Derivative Priorities

After Moody's downgraded Bank of America in 2011 by two notches, counterparties to the derivatives insuring European debt wanted the exposure moved to the retail sector of the bank where depositors entrust their money.

Bank of America holds almost $62 trillion in derivative contracts. By allowing Bank of America to commingle derivative instruments with the retail sector, the Federal Reserve exempted Bank of America from the Federal Reserve Act (Section 23A), which limits the transfer of these instruments to protect depositors and the overall soundness of the bank.[32]

---

[32] (Ivry, Son, & Harper, 2011)

Is Your Money at the Bank at Risk?

Derivatives are also given special priority status in bankruptcy proceedings, which means they are exempt from normal bankruptcy rules designed to protect debtors from creditor demands for payment. Derivative exemptions from bankruptcy rules were put in place with heavy industry lobbying under the argument that defaults on derivatives could wreak havoc on the financial system. It turns out that this exemption actually encourages the use of derivative contracts since creditors have a claim to assets regardless of bankruptcy status. [33]

The Dodd-Frank Act does little to change this priority status. The FDIC has blanket authority to pay the claims of creditors during Dodd-Frank bank resolutions. The act only requires that all derivatives with the same party be treated the same, i.e. either cancel all of them or pay all of them. It is unlikely that the FDIC will reject all derivative claims, especially when the Federal Reserve and the Treasury Department both play a major role in whether to place a company in a Dodd-Frank style resolution in the first place with ample opportunity and influence to insist that derivatives be protected.[34]

JP Morgan (JPM), the largest holder of derivatives, has almost $70 trillion in derivatives on $2.3 trillion in assets, so they are leveraged 29:1. The derivatives are also mostly held in the depository arm of the bank. This means that a 1% loss in its derivative contracts exceeds the entire market value of the company of $188 billion by four times.

---

[33] (Skeel, 2010, p. 123)
[34] (Skeel, 2010, pp. 143-144)

To put this in perspective, the FDIC has $33 billion as of December 31, 2012 to insure total deposits of over $9 trillion.[35] The U.S. GDP is approximately $16 trillion, and world GDP is about $70 trillion. Meanwhile total outstanding derivatives for the top 25 holding companies are almost $300 trillion.[36]

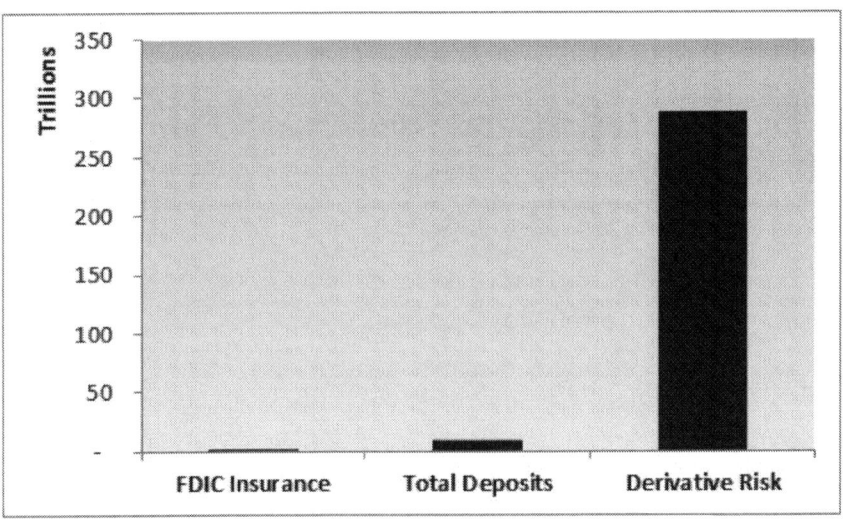

Source: FDIC, Office of the Comptroller of the Currency; U.S. Department of the Treasury

The FDIC has an additional $100 billion line of credit with the Department of the Treasury. Dodd-Frank also adds additional provisions for the FDIC to borrow from the Department of the Treasury. How will the FDIC guarantee depositor funds when derivatives have first claim to bank assets, and even small percentage losses in total derivatives amount to many times depositor funds?

JP Morgan and Bank of America alone hold over $131 trillion in derivatives. For the two banks holding the most derivatives, a 2% loss represents $2.6 trillion, or over 16% of U.S. GDP. In an

---

[35] (FDIC, 2013)
[36] (OCC, OCC's Quarterly Report on Bank Trading and Derivatives Activities Fourth Quarter 2012, 2012)

emergency similar to Cyprus, it is not unlikely that Cyprus style depositor haircuts could make up the massive shortfalls in FDIC funds likely guaranteeing derivative contracts even under Dodd-Frank provisions.

Low Interest Rates Disguise the True Risk of Bank Derivatives

Keeping interest rates low makes it appear that these megabanks are solvent as it boosts the value of its assets. A major part of the Libor scandal to lower interest rates was to give the appearance that the banks are solvent, because rising interest rates would wipe out their bad debts that they have on the books (when interest rates rise the value of debt goes down).

Many of these banks are insolvent and it is only a matter of time until the public finds out about it, accounting and interest rate shenanigans aside. Investors can short megabanks like JP Morgan (JPM) by buying a put option, where the buyer of the option has the right to exercise the contract to sell the stock at the contract price, and buy the stock at a lower price to cover the contract. If the stock price does not fall in value compared to the put option "strike" price, then the buyer of the option contract can simply forfeit the fee paid for the contract.

In times of economic turmoil, some of these contracts, however, may not be honored. Because assets values are not marked to market, nor do they properly account for losses in the derivatives market, bank stocks are prone to complete collapse.

Bank Stocks and Mark-to-Market

Under pressure from Congress, on April 2, 2009 the Financial Accounting Standards Board (FASB) voted to suspend mark-to-market rules for bank assets. The ruling allows banks to *ignore market prices for assets*. This also increased the banks' lending capacity based on newly stated capital that is no longer based on mark-to-market accounting.

This essentially means that banks do not need to report actual losses that they are incurring from bad mortgages.

Loans that should have been written down as losses or written off completely are still on the banks' balance sheets.

Changing accounting methods and central intervention does not prevent the inevitable; it only delays it. When the market discovers the true price of bank assets, then destruction comes and often without warning. Though the government and banks argue that the heart of the financial crisis is a lack of liquidity, the true nature of the problem is deteriorating asset values (loans). Plenty of liquidity is available to buy up assets, but if the banks were to sell the assets at the true asset values, asset values would plummet and bank losses would mount.

Although this process is currently being delayed with mark-to-market accounting suspension and central bank interventions, sooner or later the truth regarding the banks' toxic assets will come to light.

It also does not do much good to buy bank stocks that pay dividends if the bank itself is going bankrupt.

When the stock price is below the book value, this is not necessarily a good value investing since investors have written bank assets down below the supposed book value in consideration of the suspended accounting rules, and the stock can go much lower as the market continues to discover the true price of bank assets.

MF Global: The First and Last Warning?

The entire banking system is currently held up by highly leveraged positions based on low interest rates that boost asset prices to keep banks solvent. When interest rates rise, the entire system is in danger of failing. Only hard assets will survive this paper collapse. Brokerage and depositor funds can be taken with no warning, and no recourse.

MF Global had over $1.6 "go missing" to cover losing bets on European debt. In a Repurchase Agreement with Spain to buy Italian bonds, MF Global received the bonds at a discount. But rising interest rates required MF Global to post more funds on highly leveraged positions. When MF Global did not have the money, they raided segregated customer accounts where funds were transferred out of the brokerage without customer approval and without warning.

Segregated funds are funds that should *never* be mixed with company funds, or used for any purpose outside of the customer's approval. Not only did MF Global borrow funds from segregated accounts, but the segregated funds were outright stolen.

Can this happen to anyone? It most certainly can, and likely will, unless investors and depositors take action to protect their money from both inflation and plain theft.

Chapter 9: Bonds – Ticking Time Bombs

"Markets can remain irrational longer than you can remain solvent."
- John Maynard Keynes

The bond bull market has been running for over 30 years since 1981, and trying to time the end of it can be a dangerous game. Even Bill Gross, co-founder of PIMCO, has suffered huge losses for calling an end to the bond bull. When the Federal Reserve intervenes in these markets, it distorts information and can prolong bull markets long after they should have collapsed.

Fear Factor

Investors who don't know where to put their money resort to the "safety" of government bonds worldwide. In the United States, demand for bonds has continued even as the national debt surpasses $16 trillion. Some simple math tells us that this is not a safe investment. For example, a small increase in interest rates means that the government will have a hard time paying the interest, much less servicing the entire debt.

Federal Intervention

The central banking system controls interest rates by purchasing U.S. Treasuries, creating demand, and lowering the interest rates (called Open Market Operations). Since it does this with printed money, it increases the money supply as well, called Quantitative Easing. This creates an inflationary economic environment where bondholders will eventually demand higher interest rates to compensate for the devaluing of the dollar. It is a game that the Federal Reserve can quickly lose control of, and the QE instrument cannot be neatly put back in the economic box of tools once unleashed.

For example, even if the Federal Reserve attempted to sell bonds to reduce the money supply, interest rates will rise as demand for U.S. securities falls, and rising interest rates will destroy the bond market.

Additionally, the Federal Reserve can only maintain a hold on interest rates for so long before the market demands higher interest rates for a devaluing dollar from years of increasing the money supply.

TIPS

Treasury inflation protection securities (TIPS) were introduced in 1997, and come in five, 10, and 30-year maturities. TIPS work by applying an inflation adjustment to the principal of the bond based on the increase in the CPI. A fixed coupon rate is then applied to the adjusted principal. As inflation rises, both the principal and the interest payments increase. Similarly, if inflation decreases, the principal and interest payments decrease.

When the bond matures, investors will receive the new adjusted principal amount or the original amount, whichever is greater. TIPS come with a built in safeguard that investors will receive the original principal back, even if the adjusted principal is lower due to deflation.

For example, if a bond investor purchased a 10 year $10,000 TIPS yielding 2%, and there was no change in the CPI, the bondholder would receive two semi-annual payments of $100, or $200 total for the year. If the CPI rose by 3% the next year, then the principal would be adjusted up to $10,300, and the bondholder would receive the coupon rate of 2% based on the adjusted principal: $206 total (10,300 x 2%). The principal adjustment and interest payments are made semi-annually. When the TIPS mature bondholders will receive the greater of the newly adjusted principal amount, or the original amount.

TIPS therefore offer insurance against inflation, and when inflation expectations are low, investors can move into TIPS as a hedge against inflation at a relatively cheap price. When the market underestimates the future rate of inflation, investors holding TIPS profit because they receive a higher inflation adjustment than the market expected. This is similar to receiving greater stock returns based on low earnings expectations. These stocks typically outperform higher flying stocks with higher earnings expectations already built into the price.

Inflation expectations are calculated by comparing a similar Treasury bond to TIPS. The TIPS coupon yield is lower than traditional treasury securities because of its built-in inflation adjustment. Investors purchasing a traditional bond, on the other hand, require a premium for inflation.

If a 10-year treasury yields 2%, and a 10-year TIPS yields 1%, then the implied inflation expectation over the life of the bond is 1% (2%-1%), or the rate an investor holding a regular bond requires for inflation.

If an investor expects inflation to be greater than the implied amount of 1%, then he would purchase a TIPS bond. If an investor expects inflation to be lower than the implied amount of 1%, then investors would be better off with a regular bond. Keep in mind this is not an absolute measure of inflation expectations since the Federal Reserve's intervention in the bond market has lowered interest rates. Other technical trading factors may affect the spread between bonds as well, but it is a general indicator.

Traditionally when inflation expectations rose, investors would demand higher yields on traditional bonds as well. But the Federal

Reserve has intervened in this market, purchasing over 70% of bonds and keeping interest rates low.

TIPS should only be purchased if inflation expectations are unrealistically low.

TIPS are indexed to the CPI and typically perform better than traditional bonds when investors underestimate inflation.

The best time to invest in TIPS is when inflation expectations are low but before substantial inflation actually affects the economy.

When inflation does begin to show up in the economy, TIPS become vulnerable to losing value just like traditional bonds. The falling dollar devalues and erodes the principal and fixed income from all bonds including TIPS. Though TIPS are indexed to the CPI, the CPI understates real inflation, and this will be especially true as inflation accelerates from the massive amounts of money printing.

Shorter term TIPS are more conservative since they are not as exposed to the risk of rising interest rates during accelerating inflation, while longer-term TIPS are more exposed to the risk of rising interest rate from inflation similar to traditional bonds.

The key is not to buy TIPS to hold them for the long-term as protection against inflation, but to profit as the market underestimates inflation and sell them before inflation wreaks havoc on the dollar and bond holdings.

A good way to execute this strategy is to invest in ETF's like iShares Barclays TIPS Bond (TIP) which tracks the index of Barclay's U.S. TIPS, which consists mostly of intermediate and long-term bonds, and PIMCO's (STPZ) which has a shorter-term focus and tracks the 1-5 year US TIPS index. STPZ is not as exposed to the risk of rising interest rate because the fund consists of shorter maturities than TIP.

Both ETF's allow you to easily buy and sell your holdings and remain liquid as opposed to holding a bond.

The interest income from TIPS is taxed at ordinary federal income tax rates, but like other Treasuries the interest income is exempt from state and local income taxes.

The TIPS adjustment is taxed in the year of the adjustment as ordinary income, though a bondholder is not paid the principal until maturity. In periods of high inflation this can even lead to tax bills that are higher than the actual interest income. For this reason many investors only hold TIPS in tax-advantaged accounts like IRA's, and especially tax-exempt accounts like Roth IRA's.

Muni – Bonds

Municipal bonds, issued by state and local governments to fund capital expenditures, are exempt from federal taxes as well as the state from which the bond was issued. Because the interest paid on a muni-bond is tax-exempt, this effectively increases the return on the investment. For example, assuming a 25% tax bracket, a regular bond must have pretax yield of 5.3% to match the 4% tax-free muni-bond (Tax Equivalent Yield = Tax Free Bond Yield/1-Tax Rate). The higher the tax bracket, the higher the yield required to match the tax-exempt yield of the muni-bond.

Investors subject to the alternative minimum tax must include interest income from muni-bonds, and some retirees who are higher income earners must include munis when calculating Medicare premiums and taxable portions of Social Security benefits.

Muni-Bond Risks

The United States is not only leveraged at the federal level. Cities, counties, and states are also highly leveraged and dependent on borrowing at low interest rates for funding. When interest rates rise, these municipalities and states will also suffer huge losses because of the debt that cannot be repaid. When the bond bubble bursts, it will not only affect the federal government, but local, county, and state governments as well.

Meredith Whitney, a financial analyst who predicted the collapse of banks long before the 2008 financial crisis, describes local and state budgets as the next phase of the collapse.

She spent two years and thousands of hours with her staff analyzing the risk the financial condition of the largest states posed to the $3 trillion dollar municipal bond market. Her conclusion was that local governments, which depend on states for a third of their revenues, will be the ones to get squeezed as the states are forced to tighten their budgets. Many cities and counties will go bankrupt. Already three cities have filed for bankruptcy in California: Stockton, Mammoth Lakes, and San Bernardino.

Cities are mainly funded by sales tax and property taxes revenues, the latter of which are especially in decline due to the housing collapse.

State pension funds are underfunded by the tune of over $1 trillion. Many government pension programs have unrealistic return projections of 7.5%-8%, where real returns amount to 1-2%, especially in an era of low interest rates.

When interest rates rise, many highly leveraged cities and states simply will not be able to afford the higher cost of debt.

Recently Warren Buffet also began to terminate credit-default swaps insuring $8.25 billion of municipal debt at a substantial loss.[37]

Buffet was willing to take a substantial loss to rid his company of insuring against municipal bond defaults.

As muni-bonds are downgraded, funds that are required to invest in only AAA securities will be forced to dump them. Unlike Treasury bonds, the Federal Reserve is not there to scoop them up as the bonds are sold off.

Fund managers would likely switch to corporate AAA bonds, and there only a few of those left.

When Will the Bond Bubble Pop?

Since no one knows when the bond bubble will pop, the first step is to stay out of medium and long-term bonds. Not only do bondholders receive real negative returns in government bonds, but investors also risk a sharply declining bond market if they want to sell before maturity.

Investors can buy bonds and expect interest rates to go lower, and sell them for a profit in the short-term, but this is speculation. Speculators can flip a house and earn a profit in a bubble market, but no one wants to be the last one stuck with the houses when the bubble pops. Similarly, bondholders do not want to be stuck holding bonds when interest rates begin to climb, diminishing the value of the bonds. If a bondholder were to hold the bond, she will be paid back in increasingly devalued dollars over time, producing negative returns and even losing a percentage of the original principal to inflation.

---

[37] (Corkery, 2012)

Even when investors start thinking that the low interest rates are not worth the safety of the U.S. bond, especially in light of inflation, interest rates may begin to inch ever slowly upward. **Even small increases in interest rates can lead to large bond losses.** For example, a 10 year Treasury bond yielding 2% would have the following losses as interest rates rose:

Interest Rate	Lost Bond Value
3%	8.58%
4%	16.35%
5%	23.38%
6%	29.75%
7%	35.53%
10%	49.85%
15%	66.26%

Shorting the Bond Market

Beware of Short and Double Short ETF's

The bond market is artificially propped up by central intervention, low interest rates, and the illusion of safety. The bond market is no longer a safe investment, but investors can lose a lot more money shorting them with the wrong investment vehicles. There are a number of investment advisors recommending short Exchange Traded Funds (ETF's) to short the bond market.

These popular and widely misunderstood ETF's to short bonds, stocks, real estate, and other markets are not advisable to 99% of the investment population. Even if investors are right in the long-term trend for these markets, they will most likely lose unless they are right on a daily basis! In fact, it is mathematically likely because the fund is not designed for the long-term investor.

The reason these funds should be avoided for any period longer than one day is that these funds are *reconciled daily*, meaning performance is based strictly on daily performance rather than long-term performance.

Because of this daily reconciliation process, it is actually possible and likely to lose money on a short, double-short or triple- short ETF even as the market goes down. These funds were simply not mathematically designed to be held for longer than one day, so losses add up regardless of the long-term trend. Please read the prospectus carefully if you choose to invest in short and ultra-short ETF's of any kind. For those short ETF's held longer than a day, you are almost certain to lose money due to short-term gyrations in the market, and the longer you hold them the more money you will lose.

Two popular ETF's recommended for shorting the bond market are the Proshares Short 20+ Treasury ETF (TBF), which returns the inverse of the *daily performance* of the Barclays US 20 year Treasury index, and Proshares UltraShort 20+ Year Treasury (TBT), which is similar to TBF except is seeks to return double the inverse of the *daily return* of the index. This means investors can make twice as much if bond prices fall, but can also lose twice as much if they rise.

Short-term bonds are safer and less likely to be affected by inflation than long-term bonds, which is why investors like shorting long-term bonds with TBF and TBT.

Short ETF Example
As an example, suppose an investment fluctuates from one day to the next and ends up slightly lower from where it started over a period of ten days.

You would think that if an investor shorted this investment with a short or double short ETF, he would at least end up with some gain since the investment went down in value. In fact the investment would gradually decline in value, and over the long-term the investor would be wiped out.

Let's see why.

If you anticipated an investment to go up or down in value, and purchased a double-long or double-short ETF based on that expectation, you would lose either way with a leveraged ETF. For example, consider an investment that fluctuated daily over 10 days with an investment return up and down by 8% on a daily basis. The double-long ETF would return double the profit, so it earns 16% when the investment rises, and loses 16% when the investment falls.

Similarly, the double-short ETF gains 16% when the investment falls by 8%, and loses 16% when the investment rises by 8%.

Since the investment lost 3% at the end of 10 days after the daily fluctuations, an investor would expect the double-short ETF to have gained 6%. But this is not the case, because to profit from the double-short investment, he must also be right on the daily fluctuations as well.

Similarly, the double-long investment gained $16 on the first day. However, in subsequent days the profit diminished because the investor must be correct on a daily basis to earn a profit. The same result occurred for the double-short ETF for the same reason, for a total loss of 12.16% on both double short and double long returns after only 10 days.

Daily Investment Returns with Leveraged ETF's

Day	Investment	Investment Return	Value: Double Long	Double Long Return	Value: Double Short	Double Short Return
0	$ 100.00		100		100	
1	$ 108.00	8%	116.00	16%	84.00	-16%
2	$ 99.36	-8%	97.44	-16%	97.44	16%
3	$ 107.31	8%	113.03	16%	81.85	-16%

4	$	98.72	-8%	94.95	-16%	94.95	16%
5	$	106.62	8%	110.14	16%	79.75	-16%
6	$	98.09	-8%	92.51	-16%	92.51	16%
7	$	105.94	8%	107.32	16%	77.71	-16%
8	$	97.46	-8%	90.15	-16%	90.15	16%
9	$	105.26	8%	104.57	16%	75.72	-16%
10	$	96.84	-8%	87.84	-16%	87.84	16%

Extending this example out to six months, the investment would trade at $56.11. This is a loss of 44% on the investment.

Daily Investment Returns with Leveraged ETF's Day 180 (6 Months)

Day	Investment	Total Investment Return	Value: Double Long	Total Double Long Return	Value: Double Short	Total Double Short Return
180	$ 56.11	-44%	9.69	-90.31%	9.69	-90.31%

You would therefore expect the double-short ETF to return 88% on this investment. Instead it lost a whopping 90.31% because of the daily fluctuations *reconciled on a daily basis*. In fact, the double-short ETF performed just as badly as the double-long ETF and had no advantage with the loss on the original investment. The reason is that these accounts are reconciled daily.

Extending this example out to one year, the original investment would trade at $31.48 for a loss of 69% on the original investment.

Daily Investment Returns with Leveraged ETF's on Day 360

Day	Investment	Investment Return	Value: Double Long	Total Double Long Return	Value: Double Short	Total Double Short Return
360	$ 31.48	-68.52%	0.94	-99.06%	0.94	-99.06%

You would therefore expect the double-short ETF to return 137% (68.52% x 2) on this investment, but instead it has lost a staggering 99% at $.94 because of the daily fluctuations *reconciled on a daily basis*. Again, the double-short ETF performed just as badly as the double-long ETF and had no advantage whatsoever because of the daily reconciliation process.

Even though the example shows extreme daily volatility to arrive at these losses, the point remains that in order to profit on these leveraged ETF's, investors must be right on a daily basis. It is not enough to be right on a long-term basis or even any period beyond one day! Even if the investment is trending strongly upward (or downward depending on your investment goals), it is very rare and unlikely that an investment will not fluctuate on a daily basis with the end result being very similar.

Statistical research has consistently shown that it is better to simply have a margin account to short investments for periods longer than one day in almost any scenario, and that **these funds should not be used under any circumstances outside of daily investments**.

ETF's are investment vehicles that are highly liquid, tax efficient, and low cost, and there are plenty of ETF's that are designed for longer-term investments that work just fine for investors. But ETF's strictly designed for daily trading (reconciled daily) are just that. Long-term gains are simply no match for daily gyrations that eat up your account through the daily reconciliation process. Read the prospectus carefully to determine whether these investments are reconciled daily, monthly (typical of commodity based ETF's), or longer, and do not invest for a period longer than this time frame.

If you plan on shorting a bubble market such as the bond market, use a margin account and not an ETF designed to short the bond bull.

You can open a margin account with your broker with a regular brokerage account or upgrade your current account to a margin account. This should be a separate account from your retirement account or IRA.

Chapter 10: Dividend Stocks and the Secret of Total Returns

A cash dividend is a portion of a company's profit that is distributed to shareholders.

Research done over many decades, including during severe bear market depression era periods have shown that the best performing stocks are dividend stocks. In fact, ninety-seven percent of the total gains in the S&P 500 from 1926-2008 came from dividends, and not stock appreciation.

According to the research of Jeremy Siegel, Professor of Finance at Wharton School and Senior Adviser to WisdomTree, established companies that pay consistent dividends have consistently outperformed just about every other stock since 1926. When the S&P 500 expanded to 500 stocks in 1957, the original "tried and true companies" consistently outperformed the "bold and new" companies in just about every market sector.[38]

In fact, holding these dividend paying stocks in bear markets allowed for even higher returns over the long-term than if no bear market had occurred at all! The reason that investors were able to pick up stocks at even lower prices, increasing both dividend yields and the amount of company stock on which dividends were paid.

The truth about the stock market is that if you do not own dividend paying stocks then the odds are heavily stacked against you. Only a small percentage of market returns are from capital

---

[38] (Siegel, 2005, p. 51)

gains. Most of the returns on stocks occurred because of the distribution of dividends to the shareholders. Dividend stocks also incurred less overall risk while offering higher returns.

This is not something that Wall Street wants the average investor to know because commissions and fees are made from heavy trading.

According to Jeremy Siegel, dividend stocks offer several other advantages over non-dividend stocks:

- Dividend stocks represent stronger, more stable companies with the consistent cash flow to pay dividends.
- Dividend paying companies are willing to share the wealth with shareholders.
- Dividends reinvested protect investors from bear markets by picking up more shares on which to pay dividends in market downturns and creating more wealth for the long-term.
- Dividend stocks have consistently outperformed the market in bear and bull markets, averaging 6% during the worst bear market: 1929-1954.

Consumer staple companies did especially well in Siegel's study as large stable companies paying consistent dividends branched out internationally. Consumer staple companies also offer several advantages as the U.S. enters a deepening economic crisis: consumer staple companies are less prone to economic downturns by offering necessities such as food, soap, toiletries, and other necessities, they offer a hedge against a devaluing dollar in international markets, and provide consistent and superior returns.

The overall long-term winning sectors in Siegel's study were consumer staples, pharmaceuticals, and energy sectors.[39]

The Curious Case of Philip Morris

No other company epitomizes the findings of Siegel's study more aptly than Philip Morris. Not only was Philip Morris the number one performer in Siegel's study, achieving annual returns of nearly 20% and outperforming every stock since 1925, but it did this with the threat of competition, litigation, banned advertising, billions awarded to plaintiffs in damages, and general vilification. All of this drastically lowered Philip Morris's *earnings expectations* while increasing actual returns. In fact, Siegel's findings show that the overpricing of stocks through investor *expectations* leads to poor returns, while companies with earnings growth *exceeding expectations* offer superior returns. Add consistent dividends reinvested in the stock and these stock powerhouses outperform every other stock in every market cycle.

The key, therefore, is not earnings growth, but whether earnings exceeded expectations of earnings growth. As Siegel pointed out, even though newer companies generated more sales, earnings, and growth, the price investors paid for the stock was too high to compete in returns, resulting in lower dividend yields and fewer shares purchased through reinvesting the dividends.[40]

Companies offering higher returns are more apt to be larger, stable companies quietly paying dividends year after year outside of the spotlight of more highly anticipated and touted companies.

---

[39] (Siegel, 2005, p. 66)
[40] (Siegel, 2005, p. 26)

Lowly Stocks and High Yields

In the 1990's Philip Morris faced increasing competition from generic brands, lowering its earnings expectations. A lower stock price quickly followed. With consistent dividend payments, this increased dividend yields and allowed investors to pick up more stock at lower prices for even more returns. Philip Morris reduced its brand price to remain competitive, and earnings expectations increased again along with the stock price.

Philip Morris was then faced with a litany of litigation that threatened its earnings for years, and called into question its entire business as a going concern. Earnings expectations sank to new lows, but investors continued to receive dividends on the lower stock price, increasing dividend yield and reinvesting dividends to pick up even more stock at lower prices.

From 1925 through the end of 2003, Philip Morris outperformed every other stock in the S&P 500 by over 7%, earning average returns of 17% when investors consistently reinvested the dividends in the stock.

Philip Morris changed its name to Altria Group in 2003 but kept the ticker symbol MO. Paying a current dividend yield of 4.75%, Altria Group has increased its divided 46 times in the last 43 years.

The Power of DRIPs
Compound interest is the eighth wonder of the world. He who understands it earns it...he who doesn't...pays it.
- Albert Einstein

If you had $5,000 in savings, and assuming you could even earn 5% in savings these days, then over a period of 30 years you would have a bit more than $20,000. But if you invested the same money in a dividend reinvestment program (DRIP) that increased its dividend by just 5% each year, you would have over $2.5 million at the end of same thirty-year period.

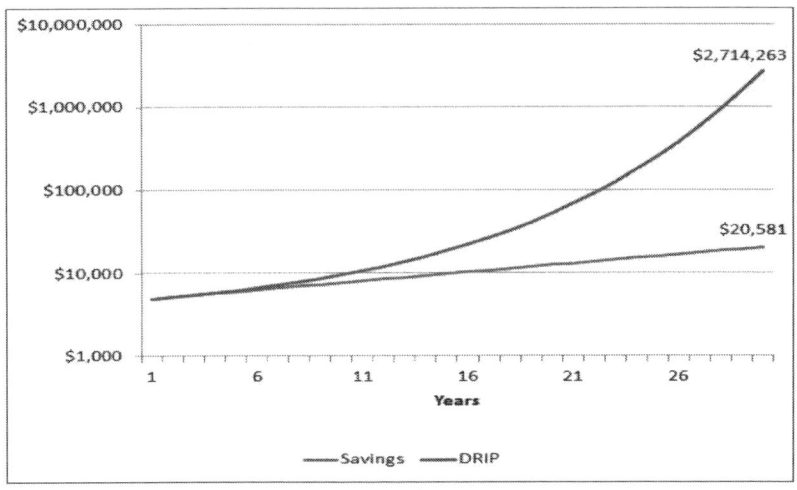

The Power of DRIPs

The key to success with dividend stocks according to Siegel's research is for investors to reinvest the dividends into the stock over the long-run. This allows the dividend payment to continue to compound. Additionally, extra shares purchased during downturns increase the overall return for long –term investors. According to Siegel, bear markets actually boost returns for those who follow this strategy because stocks are picked up at lower prices and dividend yields increase.

When investors purchase dividend stocks in companies that increase their dividend payments, they are adding even more funds that are compounded over time. The process of acquiring dividend stocks and reinvesting those dividends into more stock trumps both market downturns and even inflation over time.

The best way to reinvest in dividend stocks is through dividend reinvestment programs (DRIPs). A DRIP allows investors to pick up more shares of the company stock by reinvesting dividend payments into the stock automatically. By enrolling in a DRIP, you are purchasing more company stock with each dividend payment without placing an order, or paying a commission.

Most brokerage firms offer dividend reinvestment plans that automatically reinvest dividends into stocks. In most cases the process of enrolling for a DRIP is as simple as checking a box online for each dividend stock that you own or purchase that indicates that you choose to reinvest the dividend payments into the stock rather than receive cash payments. You will then be notified by special alerts or email when a dividend payment was made and reinvested in the company stock.

Screening Dividend Stocks

When you eliminate stocks that do not pay dividends, you are beginning to move the odds back in your favor to the 97%. You are also eliminating thousands of stocks.

As the financial collapse approaches, investors may be tempted to invest outside of the U.S. in emerging foreign markets. This can leave investors exposed to emerging markets dependent on exports to the U.S. also face collapsing economies. These economies, including Asian exporters, are even more prone to collapse since so much of their economy is export driven, while at least the U.S. has a more diverse economy and can sustain a decline in exports.

International Dividend Stocks

Combining a dividend stock strategy with companies that have substantial sales overseas hedges investors from a falling dollar as U.S. companies exchange foreign currency made abroad for devalued dollars at home, increasing profits. Many of these blue chip companies also have a substantial amount of their income generated from overseas. And additional gains mean additional dividends.

This also allows investors to invest in foreign markets without being overly exposed to foreign stocks vulnerable to declining worldwide markets.

High-dividend stocks of stable companies with a market reach well beyond the U.S. and in Siegel's long-term winning sectors include Johnson & Johnson, Procter & Gamble, and Colgate Palmolive.

Better Options for Bond Investors

Many institutional investors turn to the few AAA corporate bonds left, driving up prices and driving down yields. This is especially true as many pension funds are required to hold AAA bonds. A better approach is to buy the dividend stocks.

There are only four AAA rated companies left in America, and with interest rates held at record lows by central banks, each of these companies pays dividends that are not only higher than the 10-year treasury bond, but the average dividend yield of 3% even surpassed the 30 year U.S. Treasury Bond for the first time. These AAA companies are Automatic Data Processing (ADP), Exxon Mobil (XOM), Johnson & Johnson (JNJ), and Microsoft (MSFT).

Bonds, money market funds, and certificates of deposit pay paltry returns based on the artificially low interest rate environment. Dividend paying stocks allow investors and would be bondholders to receive higher returns in a low interest rate environment.

Holding these dividend stocks also allows investors to benefit from rising dividend payments in stable, worldwide companies.

Johnson & Johnson has raised its dividend for the past 50 consecutive years, ADP has raised its dividend for 37 consecutive years, Exxon Mobile has raised its dividend for 30 consecutive years, and Microsoft has consistently raised its dividend the past 8 years.

AAA Rated Corporate Bond Companies offering Stock Dividends

Company	Ticker	Dividend Yield	Consecutive Years of Dividend Increases
Johnson & Johnson	JNJ	3.41%	50 Years
ADP	ADP	2.94%	37 Years
Exxon Mobile (XOM)	XOM	2.57%	30 Years
Microsoft	MSFT	3.42%	8 Years

All four stocks are also in the Vanguard Dividend Growth Fund VDIGX, a well-managed mutual fund that focuses on holding high quality dividend paying stocks.

Recession Proof Dividend Stocks

Companies that specialize in necessities, that pay a dividend and that have sales outside of the U.S. are positioned to weather economic downturns. These companies include Procter & Gamble (PG), Johnson and Johnson (JNJ), Colgate Palmolive Co. (CL), Clorox (CLX), and Campbell's Soup Co (CPB).

Companies with significant revenue overseas also insulate investors from a weakening dollar.

Procter & Gamble (PG) is the world leader in personal and household products, selling its household products to over 4 billion people worldwide. It is also positioned in key growth areas in emerging markets worldwide. Its flagship products include Tide detergent, Gillette razors, Charmin, Bounty, and Pampers diapers, all household staples that insulate the company from recessions. Over 60% of its sales are international, and 38% are in developing, emerging markets, while paying a steadily increasing dividend of over 3% as of 2012.

Johnson & Johnson (JNJ) is a worldwide company with three main divisions that specialize in consumer items with $14.9 billion in sales, pharmaceuticals with $24.4 billion in sales, and medical devices with $25.8 billion in sales. Over half of its sales are in international markets, with a large portion of its consumer division focused on necessities such as oral care, baby care, skin care, and first – aid items. The stock pays a steadily increasing dividend with a yield of over 3.4%.

Colgate Palmolive Co. (CL) receives over 80% of its $16.7 billion in revenue from overseas, with double digit growth in emerging markets. With growing earnings worldwide, it also pays a steadily growing dividend of over 2.3% per share and specializes in recession proof products like dental care, household products, deodorant, soap, and other personal care products.

Clorox (CLX) is a U.S. based global company with worldwide sales of $5.2 billion. It specializes in recession proof products such as home care, laundry, cleaning and household, and personal care products. Clorox doubled its per share dividend payments over the past five years with a dividend yield of over 3%, and has global revenues accounting for over 20% of its revenue.

Campbell's Soup Company (CPB) manufactures and sells staple food items in America with sales of $7.7 billion, with plans to increase sales internationally while stabilizing growth at home. The company currently pays a dividend at 3.3%.

U.S. Companies with global sales and necessities

Company	Ticker	Dividend Yield	Overseas Revenue
Procter & Gamble	PG	3.28%	61%
Johnson & Johnson	JNJ	3.41%	56%
Colgate Palmolive Co.	CL	2.33%	82%
Clorox Co.	CLX	3.45%	21%
Campbell's Soup Co.	CPB	3.30%	30%

We are not looking for capital gains in rising stocks, but stable companies with an international reach that pay reliable dividends in diverse markets, with the purpose of reinvesting those dividends into the company stock for above average *total returns.*

Another way to pick high quality dividend paying stocks is to look over top mutual funds and ETF's with dividend stocks and invest in the funds directly, or select individual stocks in the funds that you prefer.

The Vanguard Dividend Growth Fund Investor Shares ETF (VDIGX)

The Vanguard Dividend Growth Fund (VDIGX) is a mutual fund that invests in high-quality stocks that are likely to pay dividends and have the potential to increase those dividends over time.

The fund primarily seeks a growing stream of income and invests primarily in high quality companies offering dividends with potential for long-term growth. These companies have an ability to increase earnings and dividends, and are typically purchased when undervalued by the market. The companies are primarily large-cap companies. The fund also holds the four remaining AAA companies in America, highlighted below.

The top ten holdings of Vanguard Dividend Growth Fund Investor Shares ETF (VDIGX)

Company	Ticker	Dividend Yield	Percent of

			Fund
Occidental Petroleum	OXY	2.64%	3.4%
PepsiCo Inc.	PEP	3.09%	3.2%
Johnson & Johnson	JNJ	3.41%	3.2%
Exxon Mobile Inc.	XOM	2.60%	3.0%
Target Corp.	TGT	2.37%	2.9%
Automatic Data Processing	ADP	2.95%	2.7%
Medtronic, Inc.	MDT	2.42%	2.5%
Microsoft Corp.	MSFT	3.47%	2.5%
Procter & Gamble	PG	3.28%	2.5%
IBM	IBM	1.77%	2.4%

Dividend ETF's

Dividend ETF's track dividend-yielding stocks. ETF's based on dividends alone may also include lower-quality companies that happen to pay a dividend, which results in a higher dividend yield. This includes companies that may no longer have the cash to pay dividends for much longer. Instead, look for funds that contain high-quality, international companies, and check the fund's holdings regularly. Or simply use it as a resource to pick international dividend stocks to invest in directly.

For example, if you want dividends that have consistently increased over the past 10 years, look into the holdings of PFM and VIG to select individual companies.

Vanguard Dividend Appreciation ETF (VIG)
The Vanguard Dividend Appreciation ETF (VIG) focuses on companies that have increased their dividends for ten consecutive years. The fund tracks the Vanguard Dividend Appreciation Index, a subset of the Broad Dividend AchieversTM Index Fund, which is comprised of companies that have strong balance sheets,

liquidity, solid earnings growth, and a record of increasing dividends for at least 10 years.

The top ten holding companies in Vanguard Dividend Appreciation ETF (VIG)

Company	Ticker	Dividend Yield	Percent of Fund
Wal-Mart	WMT	2.32%	4.6%
Coca-Cola Co.	KO	2.73%	4.2%
IBM	IBM	1.76%	4.1%
Chevron Corp.	CVX	3.28%	4.1%
PepsiCo Inc.	PEP	3.10%	4.0%
Procter & Gamble	PG	3.28%	4.0%
Exxon Mobil Corp.	XOM	2.59%	3.9%
United Technologies Corp.	UTX	2.53%	3.5%
McDonald's Corp.	MCD	3.39%	3.4%
3M Co.	MMM	2.47%	3.2%

Vanguard High Dividend Yield Index ETF (VYM)

The Vanguard High Dividend Yield Index ETF (VYM) tracks the performance of common stocks that are characterized by a high dividend yield through the High Dividend Yield Index. The index consists of stocks that pay dividends that are higher than average.

The top ten holdings of Vanguard High Dividend Yield Index ETF (VYM)

Company	Ticker	Dividend Yield	Percent of Fund
Exxon Mobil Corp.	XOM	2.60%	6.4%
Microsoft Corp.	MSFT	3.47%	3.8%
General Electric Co.	GE	3.64%	3.7%

Chevron Corp.	CVX	3.29%	3.5%
AT&T Inc.	T	5.21%	3.3%
Procter & Gamble	PG	3.28%	2.9%
Johnson & Johnson	JNJ	3.41%	2.9%
Wal-Mart Stores Inc.	WMT	2.32%	2.9%
Pfizer Inc.	PFE	3.67%	2.9%
Coca-Cola Co.	KO	2.76%	2.6%

PowerShares Dividend Achievers ETF (PFM)

PowerShares Dividend Achievers ETF (PFM) focuses on dividend paying companies that have increased their annual cash dividend payments for 10 or more consecutive years. The fund corresponds to the price and yield of the Broad Dividend AchieversTM Index, an index of companies that have increased annual regular dividends for each of the last ten years or more.

The top ten holdings of PowerShares Dividend Achievers ETF (PFM)

Company	Ticker	Dividend Yield	Percent of Fund
Procter & Gamble	PG	3.28%	5.0%
AT&T Inc.	T	5.22%	5.0%
Wal-Mart Stores Inc.	WMT	2.32%	4.8%
Chevron Corp.	CVX	3.29%	4.8%
Coca-Cola Co.	KO	2.76%	4.8%
IBM	IBM	1.76%	4.7%
Johnson & Johnson	JNJ	3.41%	4.7%
Exxon Mobile Corp.	XOM	2.60%	4.7%
PepsiCo Inc.	PEP	3.09%	3.1%
Abbott Laboratories	ABT	1.69%	2.9%

iShare Dow Jones Select Dividend Index Fund (DVY)

The iShare Dow Jones Select Dividend Index Fund (DVY) seeks investment results that correspond generally to the price and yield performance of the Dow Jones U.S. Select Dividend Index, a group of 100 of the highest dividend yielding securities in the Dow Jones U.S.

The fund has a more contrarian slant than other funds, and is also focused more on mid-cap stocks.

The top ten holdings of iShare Dow Jones Select Dividend Index Fund (DVY)

Company	Ticker	Dividend Yield	Percent of Fund
Lorillard, Inc.	LO	5.41%	3.5%
Lockheed Martin Corp.	LMT	4.96%	2.9%
Kimberly-Clark Corp.	KMB	3.51%	2.1%
PPG Industries, Inc.	PPG	1.69%	2.1%
Chevron Corp.	CVX	3.29%	2.0%
CenturyLink Inc.	CTL	7.35%	1.9%
Entergy Corp.	ETR	5.28%	1.8%
Integrys Energy Group Inc.	TEG	5.10%	1.8%
Clorox Co.	CLX	3.45%	1.7%
DTE Energy Company	DTE	4.08%	1.7%

SPDR S&P Dividend ETF (SDY)

The SPDR S&P Dividend ETF (SDY) holds 60 of the highest yielding dividend stocks that have raised their dividends every year for the past 25 years. The fund tracks the performance of the S&P High Yield Dividend Aristocrats Index compromised of companies that have historically followed a policy of making dividend payments. The fund has a mid-cap focus.

The top ten holdings of SPDR S&P Dividend ETF (SDY)

Company	Ticker	Dividend Yield	Percent of Fund

Company	Ticker		
Avon Products Inc.	AVP	1.54%	2.9%
Pitney Bowes Inc.	PBI	12.87%	2.6%
AT&T Inc.	T	5.23%	2.4%
HCP Inc.	HCP	4.39%	2.3%
Nucor Corp.	NUE	3.26%	2.1%
Consolidated Edison, Inc.	ED	4.32%	2.1%
Leggett & Platt, Inc.	LEG	4.22%	2.1%
Johnson & Johnson	JNJ	3.42%	2.0%
Clorox Co.	CLX	3.45%	1.9%
Kimberly-Clark Corp.	KMB	3.52%	1.8%

WisdomTree LargeCap Dividend (DLN)
The WisdomTree LargeCap Dividend Fund (DLN) seeks to track the price and yield performance of the WisdomTree LargeCap Dividend Index, which consists of large cap dividend paying stocks. This fund is based on Siegel's research that indicates balancing portfolios based on dividend yields instead of market prices alone offer superior returns.

This fund looks for the largest companies projected to pay the most cash dividends to shareholders over the next year, thereby *balancing market capitalization with dividend yield.*

The top ten holdings of WisdomTree LargeCap Dividend (DLN)

Company	Ticker	Dividend Yield	Percent of Fund
AT&T Inc.	T	5.24%	4.4%
Exxon Mobile Corp.	XOM	2.59%	3.7%
General Electric Co.	GE	3.64%	3.0%
Pfizer Inc.	PFE	3.68%	2.7%
Microsoft Inc.	MSFT	3.46%	2.6%

Chevron Corp.	CVX	3.29%	2.6%
Johnson & Johnson	JNJ	3.41%	2.5%
Merck & Co. Inc.	MRK	4.06%	2.4%
Verizon Communications	VZ	4.78%	2.4%
Wal-Mart Stores Inc.	WMT	2.32%	2.4%

Chapter 11: The Endgame: Gold and Silver

The rise in gold is not a mystery. There is a very clear and predictable relationship between gold and the weakness of the dollar. Gold retains its value, no matter how much money printing occurs worldwide. Gold, unlike derivatives, has no counter-party risk or debt.

Even the U.S. dollar has counterparty risk since it represents government debt, and may not be fully paid or honored. For example, in 1933 the government decreed that the U.S. dollar was worth $35 in gold instead of $20.67 per ounce, for an *immediate loss of 69%* on dollars held. Since 1971 when the U.S. abandoned the gold standard altogether, the losses on the dollar have only accelerated.

Gold is not debt, and therefore has no liability or counterparty risk, and will be the last bastion of safety as fiat currencies collapse worldwide.

This means that gold will continue to rise, and very likely dramatically, over the next several years.

The New Gold Rush: Investors Who Predicted the 2008 Financial Crisis are Buying Gold

We believe the market has already made gold the new reserve currency. The governments and central banks haven't officially adopted it yet, but the market has voted gold in by revaluing it upwards for the past 10 years against all paper currencies.
- Eric Sprott, Sprott Asset Management

In 2010 George Soros declared gold "the ultimate asset bubble." Either George Soros had a change of heart or is buying under the radar, because in 2012 he increased his stake in SPDR Gold Trust

(GLD) from 319,500 to 884,400. At the end of 2012, Soros's gold holding increased to 1.3 million shares. In addition to this, he more than doubled his holding in GDX, the major gold miner ETF, to 2.32 million shares according to his third quarter 13-F filing with the SEC for 2012.

John Paulson, the billionaire hedge fund manager who famously called the financial crisis in 2008 and shorted sub-prime mortgages, increased his stake in the SPDR Gold Trust ETF (GLD) from 16.7 million to 21.3 million shares by mid-2012.[41] Paulson has also been moving from ETF GLD to physical gold as counterparty risk increases during a financial crisis. When everyone wants their gold, there is no guarantee any ETF fund can provide it.

Paulson is also investing in Anglogold Ashanti Limited (AU), NovaGold Resources (NG), Allied Nevada Gold (ANV), Randgold Resources (GOLD), Agnico-Eagle (AEM), Barrick Gold (ABX), IAMGOLD (IAG), Gold Fields Ltd. (GFI), and International Tower Hill Mines (THM).

Because Paulson's investments have declined in 2012, this may add pressure from his clients to sell mining stocks and gold holdings. Though the timing of gold can cause short-term concerns, investors should buy on dips in preparation for the escalating crisis in fiat currencies. There is also some evidence that gold prices are suppressed as discussed below.

Suppressed Gold Prices and China's Buying Spree

China has been consistently buying gold as a hedge against its trillion dollar treasury holdings, but a recent leaked cable also indicates China believes the U.S. suppresses the price of gold to retain its world reserve currency status.

---

[41] (White, 2012)

"The U.S. and Europe have always suppressed the rising price of gold. They intend to weaken gold's function as an international reserve currency. They don't want to see other countries turning to gold reserves instead of the U.S. dollar or euro.

Therefore, suppressing the price of gold is very beneficial for the U.S. in maintaining the U.S. dollar's role as the international reserve currency. China's increased gold reserves will thus act as a model and lead other countries toward reserving more gold. Large gold reserves are also beneficial in promoting the internationalization of the RMB."[42]

This cable also reveals that gold is demanded internationally in an increasingly intense currency war. When the music stops and currencies collapse, those countries with the most gold will eventually come out on top.

China recently approved gold as a reserve asset, and has also become a net seller of U.S. Treasuries.

And according to the World Gold Council, central banks became net buyers of gold for the first time in 21 years in 2010.

Total quantities of physical gold purchased have exceeded total quantities of physical gold sold by central banks and other institutions.

---

[42] (Pilar, 2011)

Net Sales (red) and Net Purchases (green) of Physical Gold from the Official Sector

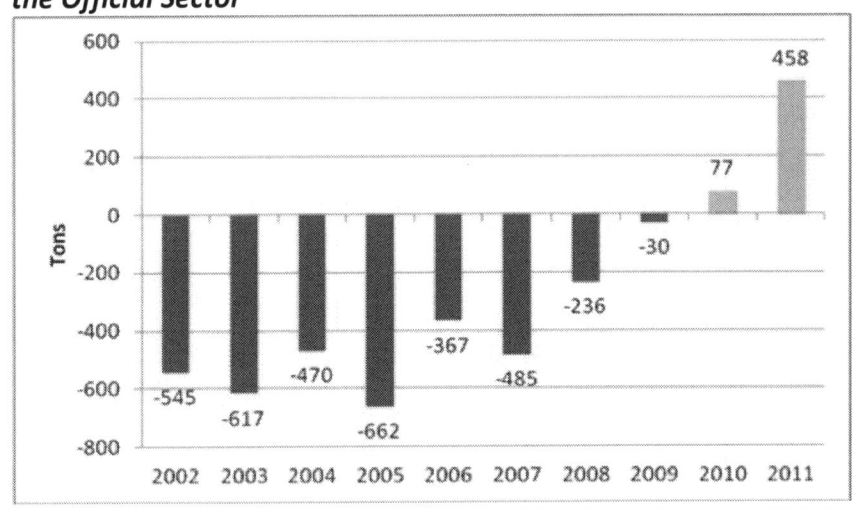

```
         600
                                                                    458
         400

         200
                                                              77
           0
  Tons                                                 -30
        -200
                                                -236
        -400                            -367
                       -470      -485
        -600  -545
                -617
        -800           -662
              2002 2003 2004 2005 2006 2007 2008 2009 2010 2011
```

The official sector is comprised of central banks and other official institutions.
Source: World Gold Council

Additionally, major investment firms like Goldman Sachs and Barclays are buying gold. Gold is increasingly valued for collateral on margin calls and loans at clearing houses and as a reserve asset at central banks and other banking institutions to increase liquidity.

The European banking system is also considering whether to add gold as a "liquid asset" for banks to meet legal liquidity requirements, which was not included in the original regulations of the EU banking regulations in spite of the fact that gold has a long history as a reserve asset for banks.

Nations Repatriate Gold

In January of 2013, Germany's Bundesbank requested 300 metric tons, or 8% of its total gold holdings stored at the New York Federal Reserve, three months after the Fed refused to conduct an audit of Germany's total gold holdings. The U.S. notified Germany that it would take seven years to comply with the request. Germany also requested 374 tons of gold that it has kept at the French central bank.

The request for gold is intended to support the German economy and the Euro, though it also signals a loss of confidence in central banks and the integrity of the monetary system. Carl-Ludwig Thiele, Executive Board Member of the Bundesbank, commented that gold held at U.S. central banks could be pledged as collateral against the U.S. dollar, which plays a key role as a reserve currency. [43]

In light of Thiele's comments, repatriating gold also places less weight on the U.S. dollar as a world reserve currency and less trust in the central banking system.

In the past few years, Libya, Iran, and Venezuela have also repatriated their gold holdings held in foreign banks.

These larger players will almost certainly put upward pressure on the price of gold as gold becomes a standard reserve currency in banks, especially since gold represents a fraction of total assets held worldwide. Increased demand from institutional buyers and central banks will have a dramatic impact on price.

The Case Against Gold?

Gold vs. Warren Buffet

Warren Buffet famously stated in his 2012 annual letter to Berkshire that gold can be fondled, but in the end it is an unproductive asset.

---

[43] (Pritchard, 2013)

Over the past twenty years, Buffet's Berkshire Hathaway increased 1,330 percent compared to gold's increase of 376 percent, or 3.5 times more. Over the past ten years, on the other hand, gold increased 416 percent while Berkshire Hathaway increased by 62 percent, or almost 7 times more than Buffet's famous investment company.

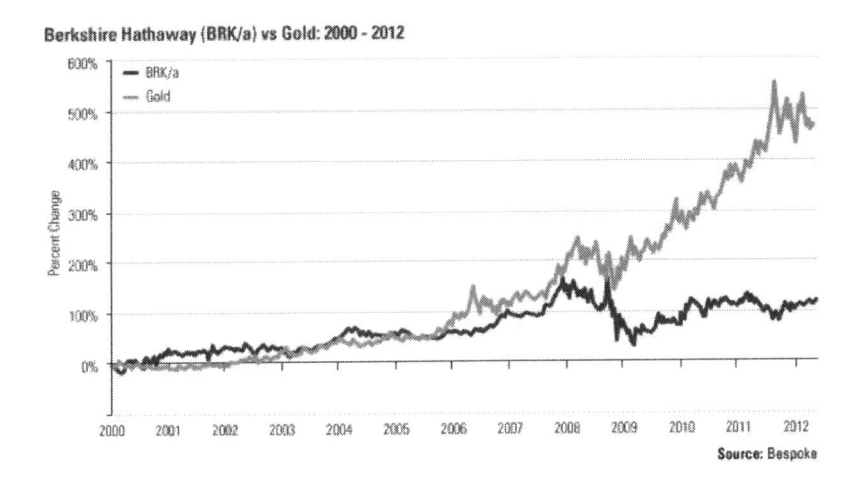

Berkshire Hathaway (BRK/a) vs Gold: 2000 - 2012

Source: Bespoke

What is important about the last 10 years, however, is that it is reflective of a financial system that has become increasingly manipulated by central bank planning, low interest rates, and excessive profits channeled to banks and other financial insiders. Warren Buffet is one of those insiders.

Gold is the canary in the coalmine that detects that something in the financial system is amiss. The continued deterioration of the financial system spurred by low interest rates and massive money printing will create more demand for gold as the last bastion of safety in chaotic and collapsing markets.

Warren Buffet the Insider

Warren Buffet not only lobbied for the bailout of banks he held large investments in, but he also invested $5 billion in Goldman Sachs after the federal government guaranteed bailouts to the investment firm. Buffet also invested $3 billion in GE on the eve of the second TARP vote, which ended up receiving $140 billion in taxpayer funding to stay afloat.

Throughout the financial crisis and bailout drama, several members of Congress were also buying shares in Berkshire stock as well as Goldman Sachs.[44] Warren Buffet has a vested interest in the current power structure that has allowed him to funnel profits his way, including through taxpayer bailout money, and corporate-government partnerships.

In fact, Berkshire Hathaway received $95 billion in TARP money from Buffet's investments in Wells Fargo, Bank of America, American Express, and Goldman Sachs. Much of Buffet's wealth comes from political relationships that allow him access to substantial government funding.[45]

The Case for Gold

Most financial advisers who called the NASDAQ bubble and the housing bubble, now believe that gold will rise spectacularly, creating its own bubble, as panicked investors flock to gold when currencies begin to fail worldwide.

---

[44] (Schweizer, 2012)
[45] (Schweizer, 2012)

Extraordinary Economic Times

Many of the experts who now recommend gold are not traditional gold bugs piling into gold as the diehard perma-bears so often do. The reason there is a confluence of agreement around gold from those who understand the economy and predicted asset bubbles of the past 20 years is that they know we are living in extraordinary economic times where fiat currencies will face historical failures, and the rush to gold will create its own spectacular rise. Like all asset bubbles, the gold prices will likely rise too high during the panics, but this is years down the road as the economies of the world recover from turmoil and failed currencies. This bubble will also pop, but we are not even close to the beginning of the gold bubble. Investors may as well ride it to the top before everyone else jumps on the gold bandwagon.

A key point in this discussion is that even those who predicted the financial crises of the past decade and do not traditionally like gold agree with traditional gold bugs at this time in history due to the precarious nature of fiat currencies. Once this crisis ends, they again diverge from their paths, some offering a gold standard as a solution, while others argue that the nature of money will continue to evolve, with the control of the money supply playing the key factor.

But investors are uniquely positioned to gain as fiat currencies fail, gold rises, and spectacularly during the coming financial disruptions stemming from artificially priced assets, collapsing currencies, and the failure of central planning.

Never before in history have nations run debts of $50 trillion, derivatives markets of over $800 trillion, and issued so much credit based on so little in assets. This is why gold, a real asset selected by the market as a store of value for thousands of years, will return as a safe haven as the rush away from credit and fiat currencies escalates. Investors will know gold is invulnerable to inflation, interest rate manipulation, and central planning mismanagement, and will rush to this proven store of value during financial upheaval and collapse.

Is Gold in a Bubble Already? Supply and Demand

In its 2010 gold report, the prestigious Erste Group's Austrian bank showed gold as a tiny fraction of total global assets held despite its twelve-year bull run. Gold investments, including ETF's and gold mining stocks, accounted for less than 1% of the total global assets in 2009.

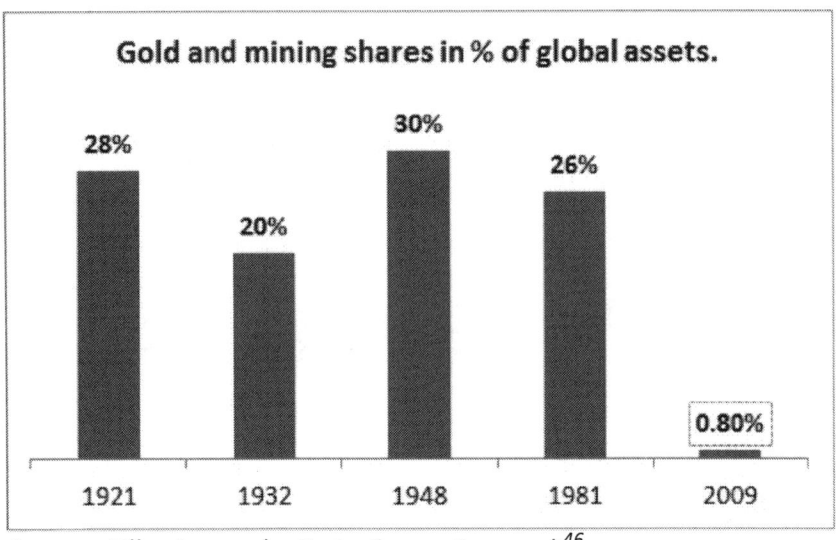

Gold and mining shares in % of global assets.

1921	1932	1948	1981	2009
28%	20%	30%	26%	0.80%

Source: Silberjunge.de, Erste Group Research[46]

According to Erste Research Group, in 2012 privately held gold amounted to $1.5 trillion, central bank holdings amounted to $1.5 trillion, and total world financial assets stood at *$231 trillion*. In other words, total gold holdings amounted to 1.3% of world financial assets as depicted in the below pie chart.

---

[46] (Erste, Gold Report 2010 - In Gold We Trust, 2010)

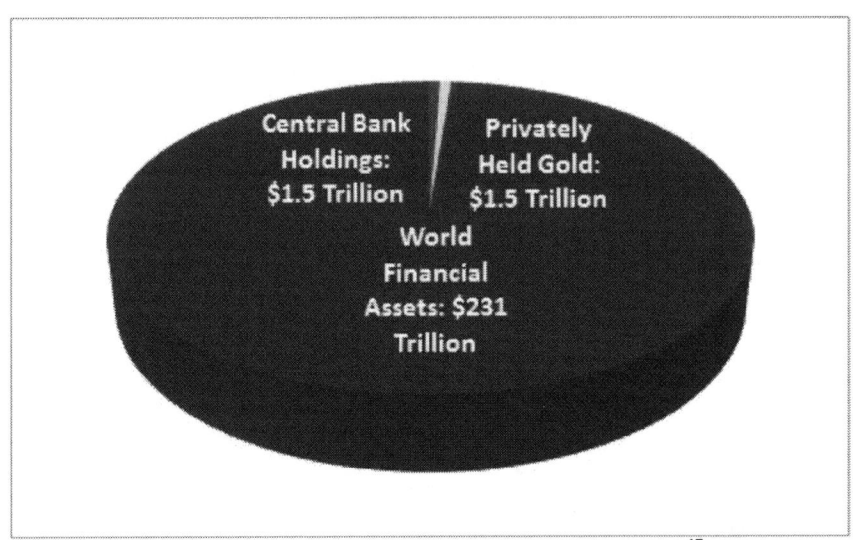

Central Bank Holdings: $1.5 Trillion

Privately Held Gold: $1.5 Trillion

World Financial Assets: $231 Trillion

Source: Bullion Management Group, Erste Group Research[47]

Even a small shift in capital from stocks and bonds into gold will have a major effect on the price of gold. As time goes by, more investors will move from unstable paper currencies and its derivative instruments into gold, and this will cause the price of gold to rise dramatically. As interest rates rise, this momentum will pick up as more assets and fiat currencies become devalued and investors scramble for a safe haven for their savings and capital.

---

[47] (Erste, Gold Report 2012 - In Gold We Trust, 2012)

Chapter 12: Paper Gold and Rigged Markets

On April 15, 2013, gold dropped by over 9%, the steepest one-day drop since February of 1983 over 30 years ago. This was after an all-time high of $1,895 in August of 2011, for a total decline of 28%.

Large paper contracts were quickly sold into the market, lowering the price of gold substantially within hours. The market opened with 100 tonnes immediately sold, followed by another sale two hours later for 300 tonnes within 30 minutes, dropping the price of gold by over $50.[48]

Over 400 metric tons of gold (12,860,298 troy ounces) were sold off in quick successions, which represents almost $20 billion at a per ounce price of $1,550 on the morning of April 12, 2013, and 15% of annual gold mine production. Only large brokerage houses like Goldman Sachs, JP Morgan, Merrill Lynch, or the Federal Reserve operating through a brokerage house, have that kind of balance to sell so many gold contracts so quickly.

The short-selling broke the $1,540 key support level, taking the price to $1,395 by the end of the trading day. This shorting strategy typically triggers more selling from other investors through stop-loss orders and margin calls which allows short-sellers to pick up contracts at lower prices (covering the short position).

COMEX futures markets are more easily manipulated by larger players, because it enables sellers to sell gold without actually owning it, called "naked shorts." These contracts typically sell at

---

[48] (Norman, 2013)

over 100 times the underlying asset[49], and it is therefore unlikely these larger sellers could deliver gold if the buyers had requested delivery on the contracts. Requests for gold delivery would expose the gold shortages in the market. The COMEX market, however, is mainly used for speculation of gold prices which are almost always settled in cash.

Large brokerage houses routinely suppress the prices of precious metals with naked shorts with no real gold or silver to back the contracts up. The futures markets are prone to manipulation through naked short selling similar to interest rate manipulation and LIBOR rigging.

According to Dr. Paul Craig Roberts, former Assistant Secretary of the Treasury, lowering the price of gold through naked short selling would also allow the Federal Reserve to prop up the dollar as the world's reserve currency. A strong gold price is an indicator that the dollar is weakening and unsound, especially while the Federal Reserve prints over $1 trillion in new dollars every year while demand for the dollar decreases worldwide. Rigging the gold markets with naked short selling allows the Federal Reserve to move forward with more quantitative easing while protecting the exchange value of the dollar. [50]

According to Dr. Roberts, the Fed also puts out word to the brokerage houses that the hedge funds will be selling off their gold holdings, who in turn inform their clients. This creates advance selling that coordinates a drop in gold prices across both hedge funds and individual investors to fulfill the Fed's purpose of surreptitiously defending the value of the dollar.

China also believes that the U.S. manipulates gold prices in order to protect the dollar's role as the world reserve currency.

---

[49] (CFTC, 2010)
[50] (Roberts, Assault on Gold Update, 2013)

Physical Gold Decouples from Paper Gold

Meanwhile physical gold dealers reported some of the heaviest buying in precious metals in years to take advantage of the lower prices, and this was occurring worldwide. [51] As gold prices slid lower, actual physical silver and gold prices crept higher in the form of higher premiums over the spot price, and buyers outnumbered sellers by a ratio as high as 50:1 according to KingWorldNews.[52][53]

As the world realizes that there is not enough gold to meet paper contracts, this decoupling of physical gold prices from paper gold will only escalate. Paper contracts, ETF's, unallocated gold, and even allocated gold not promising delivery can all be settled in cash as this process plays out. Now is the time to focus on owning and storing physical precious metals as these prices decouple from paper contracts. The following section discusses how to buy and store physical precious metals.

---

[51] (Mukherji & Nayak, 2013)
[52] (King, 2013)
[53] (Roberts, Assault on Gold Update, 2013)

Chapter 13: How to Buy Gold

Physical Gold Insures Against all Counterparty Risk

Physical gold, unlike derivatives, has no counter-party risk or debt. Counterparty risk occurs when one party does not live up to the stated obligations of the agreement.

For example, a homeowner purchasing fire insurance faces the counterparty risk that a bankrupt insurance company will not fully reimburse a homeowner. When there are a lot of fires, counterparty risk becomes multiplied. During the financial crisis of 2008, for example, AIG was unable to fulfill its obligations to pay out contracts on credit default swaps that insured investors against mortgage-backed securities (MBS) losses. AIG was bailed out to the tune of $182 billion to cover the losses.

The dollar also has counterparty risk. After all, the original purpose of the dollar was to serve as a note for gold held in storage. Since the gold anchor was jettisoned in favor of a free floating dollar, the value of the dollar can rapidly devalue. The dollar is now merely debt printed in exchange for U.S. Treasury Securities with no tangible assets backing it. There exists counterparty risk that the U.S. dollar will continue to lose value as the Federal Reserve prints money to fund the U.S. government with devalued dollars. There is also counterparty risk of bank holidays in which, during financial turmoil, the value of the dollar is devalued against gold.

Own Physical Gold

Owning physical gold eliminates all counterparty risk and claims to physical gold. There is a risk your gold is stolen, confiscated, or lost, but it cannot be devalued like fiat currency, or defaulted on like debt because gold is an asset with no debt attached to it, unlike the U.S. dollar that can be devalued through quantitative easing. Gold deprives the money changers of the power to print money and buy up assets with fiat currencies, thereby fraudulently transferring wealth. It is the truest form of money and has been for thousands of years.

In a world leveraged with massive counterparty risks through derivatives and fiat currency, gold is one of the few assets with no counterparty risk.

If gold owners choose the wrong place to store gold, they may face losses based on theft and other forms of loss if the gold is not insured. Banks have even broken into safe deposit boxes to confiscate gold, so it is not recommended that gold owners store large amounts of gold at a bank. Moreover, safe deposit boxes are not insured like checking and savings accounts.

Investors run the risk of gold confiscation, bank holidays, and theft, so larger quantities of gold should be deposited at an insured depository discussed below.

During crises scenarios, buyers will pay a high premium for physical gold, and in some cases it will not even be available. During the crisis of 2008, buyers were forced to pay a premium of 9-15% to purchase gold. The next crisis will be bigger, badder, and longer, and gold will go through a prolonged period of rising prices and at some point may not even be available at any price.

Gold on Hand

Gold owners should have some gold on hand locally and even hidden in the house or yard where only the owner and one other person know where it is located. Larger amounts of gold should be stored and insured. Nevertheless, in an emergency gold owners will only have access to what they have on hand for purchases. For those who live in a state that has recognized gold as legal tender (see below), gold owners can also deposit some gold and use an electronic system to make your purchases based on gold deposits.

Numismatics vs. Gold Bullion

Gold buyers seeking to preserve their wealth from the ravages of inflation should buy gold bullion. Collectors, on the other hand, are looking for numismatics or collectible coins. Some online dealers like to deliberately confuse the two to greatly mark up the prices on collectibles that do not have much gold. If you are an experienced collector who understands numismatics, then by all means pursue numismatics where coins can go up in value based on factors outside of the value of gold.

But for our purposes, regarding the preservation of value as a hedge against devaluing fiat currencies, we are specifically talking about gold bullion bars and coins like the American Eagle, Canadian Maple Leaf, the Australian Kangaroo, the Austrian Philharmonic, and the South African Krugerrand (1 oz. coins). Gold buyers purchasing gold based on its value in gold content are only looking for coins as outlined in the table below.

Gold is money and can be traded for food, clothes, housing, and whatever you need during times of financial crisis. Numismatics are collectors' items that may or may not be worth what the dealer says it is worth.

Primary Gold Coins and Denominations

1 Ounce Gold Coins	Percentage of Gold	Denominations
American Gold Eagle	.9166 fine (alloyed with silver and copper)	Available in 1 oz., ½ oz., ¼ oz., and 1/10 oz. coins.
Gold American Buffalos	Pure Gold (.9999 fine)	Only available in 1 oz. coins, with other sizes currently under consideration by U.S. mint.
Australian Nugget (Kangaroo)	Pure Gold (.9999 fine)	Available in 1 oz., ½ oz., ¼ oz., 1/10 oz. and 1/20 oz. coins.
Austrian Vienna Philharmonic	Pure Gold (.9999 fine)	Available in 1 oz., ½ oz., ¼ oz., and 1/10 oz. coins.
Canadian Gold Maple Leaf	Pure Gold (.9999 fine)	Available in 1 oz., ½ oz., ¼ oz., 1/10 oz. and 1/20 oz. coins.
South African Krugerrand	.9166 fine (alloyed with copper)	Available in 1 oz., ½ oz., ¼ oz., and 1/10 oz. coins.

Even though the Krugerrand is alloyed with copper and Gold Eagle is alloyed with silver/copper which reduces the total percentage of gold, all five coins contain a full ounce of gold. The alloy protects the coins from scratching and marring which helps preserve the resale value.

Fractional-ounce coins are also available though you will generally pay a higher premium than the one ounce version, but in a financial crisis these can be useful for transactions that do not require a full ounce of gold. Additionally, in a rising market you are likely to get your premium back from a reputable dealer.

Spot Prices, Premiums, and Spreads

The *spot price* is the price large institutional buyers pay for gold on large future exchanges in New York, London, and Hong Kong.

A few large multibillion-dollar bullion companies sell gold bullion at a *premium* over the spot price for delivery to major gold dealers. The gold dealers, in turn, charge a *mark-up* to cover the premium paid in addition to a small profit. If the dealer paid a premium of 3% and sells it for 5%, then the mark-up is 2%. More generally, this is referred to as a premium over the spot price to the buyer of 5%.

The spread refers to the difference between the price that the dealer is willing to buy a coin for, called the *bid price*, and the price that the dealer is willing to sell a coin for, called the *asking price*. The asking price is always higher than the bidding price and is the profit to the dealer.

In a market that is not in financial crisis or turmoil, buyers of gold should not pay more than 5% to 7% above spot for 1 oz. gold bullion coins, with higher mark-ups for more well-known coins like the American Eagle and the American Buffalo. The American Eagle and Buffalo are the only bullion coins with weight, purity, and content guaranteed by the U.S. Government. Dealers will also sell lower-denominated coins for a higher premium.

During the financial collapse, the mark-ups paid for gold bullion can increase rapidly if there are any gold coins to be had at all. During the financial crisis of 2008, it was not uncommon to pay premiums of 15% over the spot price for gold coins.

For other coins such as collectibles or memorabilia, the dealers often make their money from large spreads, selling coins at a much higher price than they buy them for because the value of the coin is not based on its gold content. Coin dealers have a lower spread on gold coins because they can be quickly sold in the market based on gold content.

Those seeking to buy gold can also buy gold coins from a local coin shop. Generally local buyers will pay a higher premium at local coin shops than online. The benefit to purchasing from a local shop is that customers will save on shipping and insurance costs.

Some states charge a sales tax for coin purchases, while other states exempt precious metals and coins from taxes. Exempt states include Arizona, Delaware, Idaho, Illinois, Iowa, Michigan, Mississippi, North Dakota, Oregon, Pennsylvania, Rhode Island, South Carolina, South Dakota, Utah, and Washington.

Other states exempt gold purchases when the total market value of a single transaction exceeds a stipulated amount. For example, California offers exemptions to sales tax when coin or bullion purchases total $1,500 or more. The table below offers a summary of various sales taxes for precious metals, though these tax laws are constantly changing and should be verified with your local tax agencies:

Sales Tax on Coins and Precious Metals

Alabama	The State charges 4% on all sales; there are also County & City taxes, which can add another 4-5%.
Alaska	No state sales tax, though local governments may still tax.
Arizona	No sales tax collected on Coins, Paper Money, or Precious Metals.
Arkansas	Sales tax is collected on Coins, Paper Money, and Precious Metals.

California	Exemption on Coins and Bullion when over $1500. Paper Money is taxable.
Colorado	Sales Tax on Coins, Paper Money, and Bullion varies by City. The State does not charge any sales tax.
Connecticut	No sales tax on Coins or Paper Money. Exemption on Bullion when over $1000.
Delaware	No sales tax collected on Coins, Paper Money, or Precious Metals.
District of Colombia	Sales tax is collected on Coins, Paper Money, and Precious Metals.
Florida	No sales tax on U.S. Coins or Currency. Exemption on Bullion when over $500.
Georgia	No sales tax collected on Coins, Paper Money, or Precious Metals.
Hawaii	General Excise Tax is collected on Coins, Paper Money, and Bullion.
Idaho	No sales tax on Coins or Bullion. Paper Money is a grey area.
Illinois	No sales tax collected on Coins, Paper Money, or Precious Metals.
Indiana	Sales tax is collected on Coins, Paper Money, and Precious Metals.
Iowa	No sales tax collected on Coins, Paper Money, or Precious Metals.
Kansas	Sales tax is collected on Coins, Paper Money, and Precious Metals.
Kentucky	Sales tax is collected on Coins, Paper Money, and Precious Metals.
Louisiana	Exemption on Coins and Bullion when over $1000. Paper Money is taxable.
Maine	Sales tax is collected on Coins, Paper Money, and Precious Metals.
Maryland	Numismatic items and Bullion are exempt when over $1000.

Massachusetts	Coins, Paper Money, and Bullion are exempt when over $1000.
Michigan	No sales tax collected on Coins, Paper Money, or Precious Metals.
Minnesota	Sales tax is collected on Coins, Paper Money, and Precious Metals.
Mississippi	No sales tax collected on Coins, Paper Money, or Precious Metals.
Missouri	No sales tax on Coins or Bullion, but taxes Paper Money.
Montana	No sales tax collected on Coins, Paper Money, or Precious Metals by the State. There is a 3% Provisional tax in some communities.
Nebraska	Sales tax is collected on Coins, Paper Money, and Precious Metals.
Nevada	Sales tax is collected on anything that sells for over 50% of its "Face Value." Private Mint Bars and Rounds are exempt.
New Hampshire	Sales tax is collected on Coins, Paper Money, and Precious Metals.
New Jersey	Sales tax is collected on Coins, Paper Money, and Precious Metals.
New Mexico	Sales tax is collected on Coins, Paper Money, and Precious Metals.
New York	Coins and Paper Money are Taxable; Bullion is Exempt when over $1000.
North Carolina	Sales tax is collected on Coins, Paper Money, and Precious Metals.
North Dakota	No sales tax collected on Coins, Paper Money, or Precious Metals.
Ohio	Sales tax is collected on Coins, Paper Money, and Precious Metals.
Oklahoma	Sales tax is collected on Coins, Paper Money, and Precious Metals.
Oregon	No sales tax collected on Coins, Paper

	Money, or Precious Metals.
Pennsylvania	No sales tax on Coins or Bullion, but taxes Paper Money.
Rhode Island	No sales tax on Coins or Bullion, but taxes Paper Money.
South Carolina	No sales tax collected on Coins, Paper Money, or Precious Metals.
South Dakota	No sales tax collected on Coins, Paper Money, or Precious Metals.
Tennessee	Sales tax is collected on Coins, Paper Money, and Precious Metals.
Texas	Coins and Precious Metals are exempt over $1000. Paper Money is taxable.
Utah	No sales tax collected on Coins, Paper Money, or Precious Metals.
Vermont	Sales tax is collected on Coins, Paper Money, and Precious Metals.
Virginia	Sales tax is collected on Coins, Paper Money, and Precious Metals.
Washington	No sales tax on Coins or Precious Metals, Paper Money is taxable.
West Virginia	Sales tax is collected on Coins, Paper Money, and Precious Metals.
Wisconsin	Sales tax is collected on Coins, Paper Money, and Precious Metals.
Wyoming	Taxes vary by city on Coins and Paper Money. Precious Metals are taxable.

theCoinologist.com

Reputable Coin Dealers

The following table is a list of reputable online coin dealers. Buyers can compare prices for coins and take shipment directly.

Miles Franklin
Provident Metals
The Coin Agent

Storing Gold Bullion

Gold Bullion should come from a reputable refiner to certify weight and purity. Even gold is subject to counterfeiting, especially when the gold market begins to take off.

In September of 2012, ten ounce gold bars bearing the stamp of the reputable Swiss Produits Artistiques Métaux Précieux showed up in Manhattan. The serial numbers and coating remained intact while the inside was drilled out and stuffed with Tungsten.

The surest way to prevent counterfeit gold bars in a rising market is to purchase gold with an unbroken chain of custody from the wholesale dealers and refiners of gold. If the chain of custody is broken, buyers should have the metals assayed before accepting them.

Buyers of gold bars will want to see the stamp of a reputable refiner. The below table shows the most well-known and accepted refiners in the gold market:

Reputable Refiners

ARG Matthey	PAMP
Argor-Heraeus	UBS
Credit Suisse	Umicore
Emirates Gold	Valcambi
Heraeus	

Large bullion bars also sell for the lowest premium. The top weights for bullion bars are 400 ounces, 100 ounces, and 32.15 troy ounces (1 kilogram).

Gold Bullion Bars

Gold Bullion	Percentage of Gold
1 oz. gold bar	Pure gold (.9999 fine)
10 oz. gold bar	Pure gold (.9999 fine)
32.148 oz. gold bar	Pure gold (.9999 fine)
100 oz. gold bar	Pure gold (.9999 fine)
400 oz. gold bar	Pure gold (.9999 fine)

Allocated Offshore Gold Savings and Storage

Storing gold offshore used to involve contacting foreign banks to arrange gold storage in safe deposit boxes, where buying the gold and then storing it were separate events that required coordinating delivery and acceptance at the bank.

Offshore gold savings programs arrived in the early part of this century to offer a convenient way to buy and store gold offshore without even leaving your home.

The following gold savings and storage services were closely vetted to offer you the best of the bunch:

GoldMoney allows you to store and insure gold and other precious metals in London, Zurich, Hong Kong, Canada, or Singapore.

Gold Money is backed by James Turk and Eric Sprott, two pioneers of the industry, and by gold mining company IAMGOLD (IAG).

Gold Money offers allocated accounts where the metals are held in the owner's name.

There is no minimum balance required, and no spread over the spot price. Rather, buyers pay the spot price of gold plus a fixed fee. This can be advantageous in a market where spreads can increase as demand for gold increases. GoldMoney also offers very competitive annual storage rates.

Paul Tustain, a former stock analyst and software pioneer, founded **BullionVault**. He took an interest in gold as protection against risky fiat currencies but found gold to be less accessible to all but the wealthiest clients. He founded Bullion Vault to bring gold to a wider customer base. BullionVault allows buyers to store and insure gold and other precious metals in London, Zurich, or New York.

Bullion Vault offers very low storage rates at only .12%, which is three times lower than even the standard ETF fee of .4% for paper gold!

BullionVault is designed to buy, sell, and store your gold. If you plan on taking delivery of your gold, the withdrawal and delivery fees are quite high: 2.5% for 400 troy ounces, and 7.5% for smaller quantities, plus transportation fees.

On the other hand, if you plan on trading gold actively, BullionVault is ideal since it offers investors the opportunity to earn the spread just like large investors when they sell gold, keeping costs low.

Both GoldMoney and BullionVault offer a good option to store your gold long-term.

Hard Assets Alliance launched on July 16, 2012, and offers fully allocated lots of gold, silver, platinum, or palladium.

Hard Assets Alliance employs Gold Bullion International, an institutional precious metals dealer offering world class storage with the LBMA (London Bullion Market Association) approved vaults for storage.

Hard Assets Alliance offers SmartMetals™ trading technology previously made only available to hedge funds, institutional investors, pension funds, and other high-net worth clients. This offers clients access to a network of 14 institutional dealers who bid against each other on both the buy and sell side which ensures liquidity and lower prices.

The Hard Assets Alliance program offers storage at fully insured vaults in New York, Salt Lake City, Zurich, London, Melbourne, and Singapore.

Hard Assets Alliance generally has higher commission fees than its competition. It offers the better choice if buyers are not actively trading gold, but simply want long-term storage and the ability to have the gold delivered quickly and easily anywhere in the world at a lower cost. The only cost of delivery is the shipping cost (UPS or Brinks).

There are no minimum order sizes for delivery or for storage.

Hard Assets Alliance does not offer options, short selling, or any sales on margin. Precious metal investors strictly buy physical metals.

Gold Switzerland was founded by Egon von Greyerz who wanted to bring gold to his private investors to protect them from the instability of fiat currencies. The firm caters to a wealthier clientele, with a minimum investment of 250,000 Swiss Francs (approx. $264,000 as of 3/2013). The firm offers storage in secure bullion vaults located underneath the Zurich airport. Each gold bar is identified with a serial number in an allocated account.

Company	Minimum Investment	Spread over Spot Price	Commissions	Annual Storage Fees
GoldMoney	None	None	.98 - 2.49% Gold 1.99 - 3.99% Silver	.12% - .18% Gold .39 - .49% Silver
BullionVault	None	.38%	.5% Max Gold and Silver	.12% Gold .48% Silver
HardAssets Alliance	None	None	1.7 – 3% Gold 3.5% or less Silver	.5 - .7% Gold .6 - .8% Silver
GoldSwitzerland	CHF 250,000 Swiss Francs	.15 - .3% Gold 1.2-3.5% Silver	.3 - .5% to sell Gold 1% to sell Silver	.65 – 1.55% Gold 1 - 1.75% Silver

Taking Delivery

The above services offer storage with an unbroken chain of custody.

Removing bullion from storage will break the chain of custody, the record of professional custody, which guarantees the gold quality to the buyer. The gold may therefore lose value unless buyers have the metals assayed before selling them to guarantee quality and purity.

It is therefore better to keep large amounts of gold in storage and insured with an unbroken chain of custody, and have gold and silver coins on hand for transactions during a financial crisis.

States Begin Accepting Gold as Currency

Utah was the first state to pass a law that recognizes gold and silver coins from the U.S. Mint as legal tender. This is the beginning of a trend in which over 12 states are considering similar laws. Since the Utah law specifies gold and silver from the U.S. Mint, this could appreciate the price of U.S. minted coins locally. These coins include the Gold and Silver Eagles and Gold American Buffalo.

The law places the value of the coin on its market value, and not the face value for purchasing power.

The U.S. coins are also treated like U.S. dollars for tax purposes, eliminating short term capital gains tax or the long-term rate for collectibles.

Other states looking to pass gold coin bills include Washington, Montana, Colorado, Oklahoma, Missouri, Iowa, Tennessee, Georgia, Indiana, South Carolina, Virginia, and New Hampshire. South Carolina and Washington are proposing using any gold coin for currency, regardless of its origin (e.g. Canadian, Australian, and Austrian minted coins). Minnesota, Iowa, Georgia, Idaho, and Indiana are also considering similar bills.

Instead of customers presenting valuable gold and silver coins for payment, and computing the worth of the coin, the Utah Gold & Silver Depository is developing a debit system that links to gold holdings in private and secure depositories (vaults). When a customer purchases an item, gold is transferred between accounts without having to remove the gold.

Leveraged Accounts

Leveraged accounts create additional risk through short-term price movements. Price fluctuations can trigger a margin call where the account holder must pay the amount borrowed due to a drop in the gold price. This can occur even if gold continues to rise in the long-term. Instead of using additional cash to cover leveraged accounts, gold buyers could continue to purchase gold during short-term dips, acquiring more gold instead of more losses.

For example, if you have $5,000 to invest, and a company offers to loan you an additional $20,000 on loan with them, you now have the ability to purchase $25,000 in gold. If you invest in gold with the loan, and the gold price drops by 15%, the company may sell out your position to protect their loan unless you send in more funds to cover the loan. This is called a margin call. If you do not send in more funds and your position is sold out, you have taken a loss of $3,750 on your original $5,000 cash investment, or 75%!

If you own the gold yourself, you are not obligated to sell, and in fact you can simply buy more gold on expectations that the long-term trend will continue. Short-term dips can eat into your profits and leave the profits with the company instead of with you. This is because in addition to margin calls, there is interest on the loan in addition to fees. An interest rate of 5% on a $20,000 loan would require a 4% return on the entire $25,000 just to break-even on the loan. An interest rate of 8% would require a return of 6.4% just to break even, and this does not even include any loan/lease fees, storage fees, or commissions.

It is almost impossible to get ahead with many of these leveraged accounts unless you happen to buy gold going straight up with no short-term dips. This is highly unrealistic.

Leveraged accounts position you for losses during short-term dips. Instead, you could be profiting from the rise in gold by buying more physical gold during short-term downtrends instead of being forced to sell out your positions to cover the loan and covering interest and other fees.

Paper Gold

ETF's

Gold ETF' (exchange-traded funds) are similar to mutual funds in that they hold a basket of stocks or commodities for a market index or industry, but they trade like stocks which makes them highly liquid. You can buy them with a mouse click, short them, set price limits and stop-loss orders just like a stock.

Gold ETF's offer investors a convenient and inexpensive way to invest in gold. The two most popular gold ETF's are the SPDR Gold Shares Trust (GLD) and the iShares Gold Trust (IAU). The ETF GLD tracks to one-tenth of the price of gold and is the largest and most liquid gold ETF. It charges a .40% maintenance fee every year. The iShares Gold Trust (IAU) tracks to one 100th of an ounce of gold and is the lowest cost gold ETF at .25% per year.

The advantages of gold ETF's are that you can invest in gold quickly in the equities market with commissions only charged by your brokerage account without the premiums and storage fees charged for owning physical gold. The major drawback to ETF's is that you do not own physical gold, and therefore you are not assured of delivery in the case of a currency crisis. ETF's are typically paid in cash. Second, it is not clear how much gold the ETF's actually hold. As the GLD Prospectus states,

"Gold bars allocated to the Trust in connection with the creation of a Basket may not meet the London Good Delivery Standards and, if a Basket is issued against such gold, the Trust may suffer a loss. Neither the Trustee nor the Custodian independently confirms the fineness of the gold bars allocated to the Trust in connection with the creation of a Basket. The gold bars allocated to the Trust by the Custodian may be different from the reported fineness or weight required by the LBMA's standards for gold bars delivered in settlement of a gold trade, or the London Good Delivery Standards, the standards required by the Trust. If the

Trustee nevertheless issues a Basket against such gold, and if the Custodian fails to satisfy its obligation to credit the Trust the amount of any deficiency, the Trust may suffer a loss."

In other words there is no guarantee as to the quality or even the quantity of the gold, and it exonerates any custodian contracted out to hold the gold of any liability or shortage of gold except for negligence or bad faith.

Moreover, only major institutional investors, investors who have invested $15 million or more, or other "authorized participants" are allowed to redeem shares for gold. Regular shareholders do not have any rights of redemption.[54]

ETF's offer a highly efficient mechanism to ride out the gains in gold and cash out, but for the endgame when only physical gold wins, buyers will need to have physical gold on hand or safely stored. The counterparty risk to gold ETF's is simply that the gold being tracked is not of the quality or even the quantity priced into the ETF. Finally, there are no rights of redemption for the majority of regular shareholders.

Better Options – Allocated Gold Funds

Central Fund of Canada (CEF)

The Central Fund of Canada is an investment holding company that invests in allocated, segregated, unencumbered gold and silver bullion held in underground vaults at the Canadian Imperial Bank of Commerce. Over 95% of the fund's assets are gold and silver bullion. The Central Gold Trust (GTU), on the other hand, invests exclusively in gold.

Both funds, which represent real ownership of allocated precious metals, can be included in most regulated U.S. accounts.

---

[54] (Fontevecchia, 2011)

As a passive foreign investment company (PFIC), gains may qualify for 15% capital gains treatment (15% for most income earners and 20% for those making over $400,000 single/$450,000 married as of 2013) instead of the collectible rate of 28% applied against precious metal ETF's and coins.

See your tax advisor about filing form 8621 to make a Qualified Electing Fund (QEF) election that allows gains realized on sales held for one year or more to be taxed at the long-term capital gains rate.

The main disadvantage of holding gold and silver in the Central Fund of Canada is the higher premium that is similar to purchasing physical bullion.

Sprott Physical Gold Trust (PHYS)

Bridging the gap between ETF's not guaranteed by physical gold and owning actual physical gold bullion is the Sprott Physical Gold Trust (PHYS). This closed-end trust fund is 100% backed by *allocated* physical gold stored at the Royal Canadian Mint. The Sprott Physical Gold Trust offers the convenience of stored allocated physical gold by allowing investors to invest in the trust instead of storing the physical gold yourself. Oftentimes the premium is also lower than buying physical gold.

The Sprott Physical Gold Trust likely qualifies for investment in your tax-deferred traditional IRA or tax-exempt Roth IRA. Check with your broker for more information.

If you are investing in a taxable brokerage account, consider filing form 8621 to make a Qualified Electing Fund (QEF) election that allows gains realized on sales held for one year or more to be taxed at the long-term capital gains rate (15% for most income earners and 20% for those making over $400,000 single/$450,000 married as of 2013) instead of the collectible rate of 28% applied against precious metal ETF's and coins.

Owning allocated gold is crucial because physical gold prices will likely *decouple* from quoted spot prices as the world realizes that: 1). there is not enough physical gold to meet real demand; 2). a gold run where investors demand physical delivery of gold from ETF's and futures contracts will more than likely be settled in cash during financial disruptions. To insure against this counterparty risk of paper gold, use only allocated accounts for gold investments (like PHYS), take possession of precious metals, and store larger amounts of gold in an insured and allocated storage vault.

Gold Mining Stocks

Gold mining stocks enable investors to leverage their investment because, as many gold analysts say, buying gold in the ground is cheaper than buying it above the ground. Many gold mining stocks also come with the added benefit of dividend payments.

Gold mining stocks offer leverage because when gold goes up the gold mining stock can go up faster when operating costs remain constant, increasing profit margins by even more, and directly impacting the stock price.

For example, when gold rises from $1,000 to $1,500, that represents a 50% increase in the price of gold. But for a gold mining company, this represents a much greater increase in operating profits with expenses constant, which in turn increases the stock price through leverage.

Leverage and Gold Mining Stocks

Increase in Revenue vs. Profits	Year 1	Year 2	**Percentage of Increase**

Revenue	1,000	1,500	50%
Operating Expenses	600	600	0%
Operating Profit	**400**	**900**	**125%**

But investors cannot pick gold mining companies without some due diligence. Several factors are taken into account, such as the amount of proven and likely gold reserves, the cost of getting the gold, the location of the gold mines, and the management of the company.

There are three tiers of gold stocks that investors should be aware of, and four if you count exploratory companies that do not own any gold but have set up shop to go find it.

Tier 1 - Senior level gold producers
Goldcorp (GG), Newmont Mining (NEM), Barrick Gold Corp. (ABX), Gold Fields Ltd (GFI), AngloGold Ashanti Ltd. (AU), Agnico-Eagle Mines Ltd. (AEM), and Kinross Gold (KGC) are examples of large and stable gold mining companies that pay dividends. These companies have large amounts of gold reserves, so when investors buy these companies they are betting that the price of gold is going to go up more than what is priced into the stock, and that these price increases can be leveraged through increased profits. Investors are not buying these companies expecting major new gold discoveries.

Gold mining stocks should also be un-hedged, as noted below, and these senior level gold producers should make up the foundation of a gold stock portfolio.

Tier 2 - Mid-tier gold mining companies like IAMGOLD (IAG), Harmony Gold Mining (HMY), and Allied Nevada (ANV) are mid-sized stocks. These companies tend to have fewer producing mines than their larger senior counterparts, and are therefore more likely to be off of the larger institutional investors' radars. These companies offer more stability than junior mining

companies with the added possibility that a producing mine can still be discovered before the investment community takes notice.

Tier 3 – Junior Mining Companies have smaller reserves but are in the production phase. Examples of junior mining companies are Golden Star Resources (GSS) and Taseko Mines Ltd. (TGB).

Exploratory Stage – Highly Risky

Exploratory stage mining companies like Paramount Gold and Silver Corp. (PZG), are the riskiest of the bunch since they do not actually own gold and there is never any guarantee that their drilling efforts will lead to a productive mine.

A gold investor's gold mining portfolio should be spread across each tier based on risk tolerance, but an allocation of 40:30:20:10 across each tier from conservative to exploratory tiers is common. Total gold investments should range from 10-30 percent (physical gold holdings plus mining stocks), with more aggressive investors weighing even higher.

Hedging
Hedging occurs when gold miners lock in the price they will sell gold for when there is uncertainty in the market. As gold continues to rise, many gold mining company heads will no longer feel the need to hedge against the risk of dropping gold prices, thereby creating more profits based on the market prices. Barrick Gold Corp. has been a notorious hedging company that has unwound all of its hedged positions as of 2009 as the price of gold continues in a long-term upward trend.

In a rising gold market, investors should avoid hedged mining companies that have already locked in the price for which they must sell their gold.

Most of the major gold miners have eliminated their hedged positions to expose their mined gold to market prices only.

Holders

Some companies also hold on to gold instead of selling all of it after production, thus further increasing the value of the company in rising markets. Two examples of companies that hold gold after production are GoldCorp (GG) and IAMGOLD (IAG). In a rising gold market, investors will want to own shares of companies that maximize the upside by holding gold and selling it.

Gold Mining ETF's

Simple ways to buy senior level gold mining stocks are through ETF's such as Market Vectors Gold Miners Index ETF (GDX). The top ten holdings make up almost 70% of the fund. The fund also includes a few silver mining companies like Silver Wheaton Corp.

The top ten holdings of Market Vectors Gold Miners Index ETF (GDX)

Company	Ticker	Dividend Yield	Percent of Fund
Barrick Gold Corporation	ABX	2.31%	12.7%
Goldcorp, Inc.	GG	1.60%	11.6%
Newmont Mining Corp.	NEM	3.10%	8.6%
Yamana Gold Inc.	AUY	1.50%	5.6%
Agnico-Eagle Mines	AEM	1.72%	5.6%
Silver Wheaton Corp.	SLW	0.76%	5.3%
Kinross Gold Corp.	KGC	1.65%	5.0%
Anglogold Ashanti Limited ADR	AU	1.90%	4.8%
Eldorado Gold Corp.	EGO	--	4.7%
Randgold Resources Ltd ADR	GOLD	0.42%	4.6%

Market Vectors Junior Gold Miners ETF (GDXJ) invests in the stocks of small and mid-cap gold and silver mining companies. The fund is reconstituted quarterly and often results in new holdings within the fund.

ETF's offer more diversified exposure to many gold mining companies instead of one individual miner.

Resource Streaming Companies

Resource streaming companies provide financing to mining companies that risk large capital expenses to bring gold into production. In return, resource streaming companies have the right to purchase high margin revenue streams on production volumes. Examples of resource streaming companies include Silver Wheaton (SLW) (discussed below), Franco-Nevada Corporation (FNV), and Sandstorm Gold (SAND). Resource streaming companies have generally outperformed mining companies due to their ability to acquire precious metals at lower fixed costs.

Chapter 14: Covering Both Bases with Silver

Not only has silver been a long-time companion of gold as a currency throughout history, but it is also valued as an industrial commodity, especially because of its superior electrical and thermal conductivity which is used for conductors, switches, and fuses. Silver is also strong, malleable, and ductile. Silver can also endure extreme temperatures and has a high reflectance of light. For these reasons, silver has been used for electronics, photography, mirrors and optics, cell phones, computers, solar panels, and even washing machines and medical purposes for its germicidal effects.

Although some silver is recycled, much of it is lost through its use in various industries, which creates even more shortages and demand. For example, at the beginning of the 20th century, there was an estimated 12 billion ounces of silver in the world. Today there are only about 780 million ounces of silver mined each year and 600 million ounces of silver held by ETF's and other investment holdings. Much of the industrial consumption of silver occurred in the 20th century and was eradicated completely. Before this time silver was mainly used for jewelry and money. Unlike gold, which tends to stay in circulation, much of the silver that is mined with gold is consumed and lost forever.

Investing in silver combines two powerful trends: silver as a hedge against fiat money similar to gold, and silver as an increasingly rare commodity.

Often referred to as "poor man's gold," the price of silver tends to be more volatile than its gold counterpart. When gold rises against the dollar, silver tends to rise with it, but even faster, and in periods where gold drops in value, silver tends to drop even faster. In this way you can leverage the price of gold by purchasing lower priced silver.

Increasingly industrialized nations are placing pressure on silver as a commodity for more cell phones, autos, and electronics. If demand increases for electronics and industrial products worldwide, especially in developing BRICS nations, silver will rise as a commodity. If fiat currencies are devalued and even collapse, silver will rise as a precious metal with monetary value.

Manipulated Silver Markets

"Silver markets have been subjected to repeated attempts to influence prices. There have been fraudulent efforts to persuade and obviously control that price."
- Bart Chilton, CFTC Commissioner

With so much demand for silver, investors have wondered why the precious metal has been fluctuating around $20 - $30 an ounce for over a year.

Recently much of silver's volatility is affected by margin where large investment banks short paper silver without actually holding physical silver (called naked shorts).

This is done on the Commodity Exchange (COMEX) futures market. The futures market has many buyers and sellers who have no intention of actually owning the physical metal. They simply buy and sell paper contracts. However, if a buyer comes into the market with the intention of taking physical possession, then the sellers must meet the demand with physical silver instead of selling the contract. Since there is very little silver in the world to meet these contracts, the price of silver would skyrocket if enough buyers required physical delivery.

Uncovered silver positions amount to billions of dollars in silver, and based on silver supply alone there is simply not enough silver to actually cover these positions. The banks that owe their customers billions of dollars holding long silver positions would have to buy the silver to fill these positions requiring delivery. But most of these contracts are settled in cash and used for speculation only.

Investment banks like JP Morgan can flood the market with sell orders even though there is no silver to back the order up. The orders are merely paper contracts to suppress prices, though the banks still owe physical silver to its customers and investors who want to take delivery.

Many of these sell orders trigger a cascading effect as investors have put in place stop losses and sell orders when the price of silver drops to a certain point.

Once the price of silver drops from these massive sell orders that trigger more selling, often executed through high-frequency trading in a matter of milliseconds, many of the sell orders can then be taken off the market, and JP Morgan and other brokerage houses can then cover their short positions and even buy physical silver at the lower price.

If a massive futures contract holder or all of these customers and investors demanded physical delivery on the contracts, however, it would crash many sellers' positions in the silver market since they would not be able to deliver on all of their futures contracts.

Jeffrey Christian, founder of CPM Group, acknowledged at a Commodity Futures Trading Commission (CFTC) hearing that precious metals trade in the multiples of 100 times the underlying physical assets.[55]

---

[55] (CFTC, 2010, p. 288)

This essentially means that for every 100 investors who trade gold or silver on the futures market, only one actually possesses the physical metal. If a default occurred in the COMEX market it would set off a financial tremor where the music stops and 100 investors are left with paper confetti in the form of IOU's that are worth nothing, and only a few investors are left holding the actual physical metals.

There is simply not enough silver and gold in the world to fulfill all of these paper contracts.

It is also in the interest of the United States that alternative forms of money like gold and silver are suppressed, because rising gold and silver prices signal that the dollar is weakening, and investors would require higher interest rates which the government simply cannot afford. The Federal Reserve can supply its agents in the futures market with unlimited funding to cover short positions since it controls the money.

Using Manipulated Markets to Your Advantage

The advantage given to smaller investors during these market manipulations in both silver and gold is that those who buy physical silver and gold now are buying them at prices that are *artificially suppressed* by investment banks, brokerage houses, and the Federal Reserve itself. These firms have billions of dollars to manipulate paper markets through naked short sales and high-frequency trading, but the smart investor can then buy *physical* gold and silver at these lower prices.

As demand for physical precious metals increases, physical gold prices will likely separate from quoted prices as investors witnessed when gold and silver dropped in April of 2013. One ounce silver coins, for example, began to sell for 25% premiums over the lower spot price, essentially filling the gap from the paper price drop as demand increased.

Once the paper charade of naked short selling and paper markets eviscerates and market demand for gold and silver escalates, those holding actual physical gold and silver will stand in a much stronger financial position as banks are no longer able to manipulate physical prices.

Own Physical Silver

The one ounce silver coins are convenient for local storage and can also be easily hidden, and made available for bartering during a currency crisis.

Silver Coins and Denominations

1 Ounce Silver Coins	Percentage of Silver	Denominations
American Silver Eagle	Pure Silver (.9999 fine)	1 oz. only
Canadian Silver Maple Leaf	Pure Silver (.9999 fine)	1 oz. only
Silver Austrian Vienna Philharmonic	Pure Silver (.9999 fine)	1 oz. only

Though investors may pay a higher premium for silver coins, premiums can be earned back when sold.

Buying silver bullion bars gives investors the most silver for the money with lower mark-ups and premiums. 100 oz. bars are more popular for home storage and safes, while 1,000 oz. bars can be stored offsite in an insured vault along with more expensive gold bars.

Silver Bullion Bars

Silver Bullion	Percentage of Silver
1 oz. silver bar	Pure Silver (.9999 fine)
10 oz. silver bar	Pure Silver (.9999 fine)
100 oz. silver bar	Pure Silver (.9999 fine)
1,000 oz. silver bar	Pure Silver (.9999 fine)

Junk Silver

Quarters and dimes minted before 1965 were made of silver. These coins trade many times over the face value of the coin, and the difference will only increase as inflation escalates.

Often the term used to describe silver coins is "junk silver," because they are not valued as collectible coins. These coins are valuable for one reason: silver content. The coins are 90% silver, and are denominated in dollars, half-dollars, quarters, and dimes.

Some precious metals dealers offer bags of "junk silver" for prices far below the premium paid over spot prices for new coins. For example, a bag of junk silver, typically consisting of quarters and dimes, contains 715 ounces of silver. Buyers typically pay for the silver content with a premium of 2.5% to 3% over spot price of silver, which is far below the premium paid for newly minted coins. As economic instability increases, the premium paid for these coins will likely increase as well.

These coins are in small denominations which make it easy to barter, and are also easily recognized as U.S. minted coins, so there value will continue to increase during periods of inflation as a viable option to debased currencies.

Pre-1965 minted coins should be separated and stored for the silver content, which will continue to rise in value as the Federal Reserve debases U.S. currency. In fact, the main reason silver was taken out of these coins was for the purpose of debasing the currency further. The government knows that savers will take coins off the market that are more valuable than the face value, which is exactly what happened.

Spend your fiat money on necessities that you can store, like storable food, batteries, household supplies, etc. These items will become much more expensive as the dollar devalues. Additionally, imported items will skyrocket, so if you have a favorite wine or other items that are typically imported, buy them sooner rather than later and store them.

Silver Mining Stocks

Senior Level Silver Stocks

Silver mining stocks, similar to gold mining stocks, offer the advantage of leverage during times of increasing silver prices because when silver prices rise, net profits can rise faster when operating costs remain constant, directly impacting the stock price.

Examples of major silver mining stocks are Silver Wheaton Corp. (SLW) and Pan American Silver (PAAS), both senior level silver mining companies headquartered in Vancouver, Canada. Both companies offer un-hedged exposure to silver, strong operational performance, and dividends. Silver Wheaton leverages the price of silver by purchasing silver from mining companies for as little as $4 an ounce, essentially keeping its operating costs for silver production fixed.

Pan American Silver is the second-largest primary silver mining company in the world, followed by Fresnillo PLC, which is headquartered in Mexico (FNLPF).

Mid to Senior level silver mining companies include First Majestic Silver (AG) based in Vancouver and Coeur d'Alene Mines (CDE) based in Idaho.

Mid-Level Silver Mining Stocks

Mid-level silver mining stocks include Endeavour Silver Corp. (EXK) with operations in Mexico, Silvercorp Metals (SVM) operating primarily in China, Hecla Mining (HL) operating in Alaska and Idaho, Silver Standard (SSRI) operating worldwide.

Junior Silver Mining and Exploratory Stocks

Junior mining companies have smaller reserves and are in the production phase. These companies include Fortuna Silver Mines Inc. (FSM) operating in Peru and Mexico,
Great Panther Silver (GPL) operating in Mexico, and Revett Minerals Inc. (RVM) operating in Montana.

Tahoe Resources Inc. (TAHO) is a larger mining company but in the exploratory phase for silver.

Silver Miner ETF's

A simpler way to leverage the rising price of silver with silver mining stocks is to buy the Global X Silver Miners ETF (SIL).

SIL has both large cap and mid-cap level stocks, and even a few juniors. The fund seeks to track the yield and performance of the silver mining industry. The top ten holdings of the ETF make up over 70% of the fund.

The top ten holdings of the Global X Silver Miners ETF (SIL)

Company	Ticker	Dividend Yield	Percent of Fund
Industrias PeÃ±oles, S. A.B. de C. V.	IPOAF	--	12.7%
Silver Wheaton Corp.	SLW	0.76%	12.1%
Fresnillo PLC	FNLPF	3.89%	11.8%
Pan American Silver Corp	PAAS	1.06%	8.3%
Polymetal International PLC	POYYF	0.59%	5.4%
Hecla Mining Company	HL	1.55%	4.7%
Tahoe Resources, Inc.	TAHO	--	4.7%
First Majestic Silver Corp.	AG	1.90%	4.6%
Hochschild Mining PLC	HCHDF	0.91%	4.5%
Coeur D'Alene Mines Corp.	CDE	0.42%	4.2%

  The silver mining ETF offers more diversified exposure to many silver mining companies instead of one individual miner.

Investors can also use the ETF to view silver mining companies to purchase individually.

Silver ETF's

Similar to gold ETF's, the iShares Silver Trust ETF (SLV) tracks the price of silver.

Silver ETF's are fine to save in premium and storage fees and take advantage of the upside of silver, but as the nation draws closer to the endgame of the collapsing dollar, investors should shift to taking *physical possession* of all precious metals, including silver.

The iShares Silver Trust Prospectus (SLV) makes it clear that there is no guarantee that investors will receive or even own physical silver, but that the fund is merely a "simple and cost-effective means of making an investment *similar* (emphasis added) to an investment in silver."

Allocated Silver Funds

Sprott Physical Silver Trust (PSLV)

The Sprott Physical Silver Trust (PSLV), similar to its gold counterpart PHYS, is a closed-end trust where each share is backed by audited and allocated ounces of silver and stored at the Royal Canadian Mint. It offers the convenience of an ETF without having to store silver bullion, but is also 100% backed by allocated silver.

The fund offers similar tax advantages to U.S. investors as the gold (PHYS) fund as long as investors timely file a form 8621 to make a Qualified Electing Fund (QEF) election. The QEF election allows gains realized on sales held for one year or more to be taxed at the long-term capital gains rate (15% for most income earners and 20% for those making over $400,000 single/$450,000 married as of 2013) instead of the collectible rate of 28% applied against precious metal ETF's and coins.

Just as spot gold prices will likely decouple from paper gold prices as the world realizes that there is not enough physical gold to meet demand, silver is even more prone to this happening as an industrial commodity and monetary metal, as the world realizes there is not enough physical silver to meet the demand in ETF's and paper contracts.

It is therefore crucial during the endgame that you hold *allocated* silver and gold. The Central Fund of Canada (CEF) also invests in allocated, segregated, unencumbered gold and silver bullion.

Chapter 15: Platinum

Platinum is the rarest of the precious metals. Like gold, platinum is resistant to corrosion, tarnishing, and oxidation. Not only is platinum rarer than gold, but it is used more extensively in industry, consuming the much smaller portions mined. Only 5 to 6 million troy ounces of platinum are mined annually.

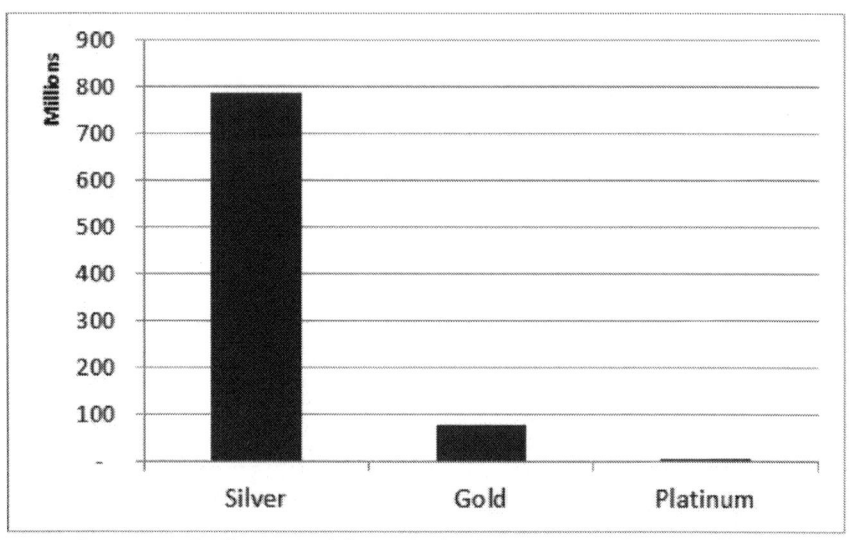

Troy Ounces of Silver, Gold, and Platinum mined annually

Platinum Demand

Platinum is used heavily in the automotive industry for emission control devices such as catalytic converters, consuming over 40% of annual platinum production. Often called "white gold," another 40% is used for jewelry for its durable nature and lustrous silvery-white appearance. Platinum is also used in industry for use in chemical reactions, electrical components, medical and dental applications, and for optical fibers and liquid crystal displays in glass manufacturing. In fact, the use of platinum in industry consumes 90% of the amount of platinum mined annually, leaving only 10% for investments.

Additionally, increased demand for clean burning automobiles worldwide, especially in BRICS nations like China and India, will increase demand for emission control devices and platinum.

The high demand and relatively low production of platinum makes this precious metal highly valued in the market. Because platinum is a much smaller market than gold, it is also more volatile.

Platinum to Gold Spread

Platinum is 30 times rarer than gold, and has historically traded at a premium to gold (referred to as "rich man's gold").

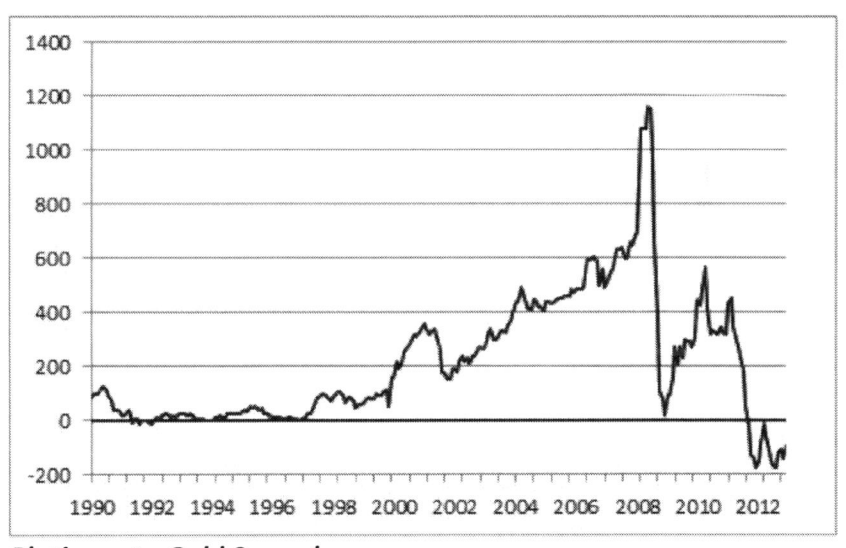

Platinum to Gold Spread

More recently platinum has traded at a discount to gold for the first time since 1991. Platinum traded slightly under gold at $1,600 ounce at the end of 2012, making it a good buy opportunity with increased demand worldwide.

Platinum can be purchased in 10 oz. bars and one ounce coins, with smaller denominations offered for the American Eagle platinum coin.

Platinum Coins and Denominations

1 Ounce Platinum Coins	Percentage of Platinum	Denominations
Platinum American Eagle	Pure Platinum (.9995 fine)	Available in 1 oz., ½ oz., ¼ oz., and 1/10 oz. coins.
Platinum Canadian Maple Leaf	Pure Platinum (.9995 fine)	1 oz. only

Platinum Bullion Bars

Platinum Bullion	Percentage of Platinum
1 oz. Platinum bar	Pure Platinum (.9995 fine)
10 oz. Platinum bar	Pure Platinum (.9995 fine)

Chapter 16: Palladium

A platinum group metal, palladium is a silvery-white, ductile metal that is less dense and has a lower melting point than platinum. It is also in great demand in industry for use in jewelry, electronics, dentistry, and surgical instruments. It's mainly in demand as an industrial catalyst, with over half of its supply used for catalytic converters.

The main difference between platinum and palladium for auto-catalysts is that palladium costs less and is used as a lower-cost alternative for lower-temperature exhausts used in diesel engines. Platinum is more expensive and must be used in catalytic converters for higher temperature, gas burning engines. Currently diesel engines are also the fasted growing engines worldwide, creating more demand for palladium.

Palladium has not had a traditional monetary use like the other precious metals, especially silver and gold, though it is still recognized as currency internationally. In fact, the U.S. recently passed the *American Eagle Palladium Bullion Coin Act of 2010* to mint the one ounce palladium coin for the first time.

Additionally, the tightening emissions control standards in Europe, Japan, China and India in the auto industry makes this rare precious metal attractive for its industrial demand as well.

Palladium Coins and Denominations

Palladium Bullion	Percentage of Palladium
1 oz. Palladium bar	Pure Palladium (.9995 fine)
10 oz. Palladium bar	Pure Palladium (.9995 fine)

Palladium Bullion Bars

1 Ounce Palladium Coins	Percentage of Palladium	Denominations
Palladium American Eagle	Pure Palladium (.9995 fine)	1 oz. only
Palladium Canadian Maple Leaf	Pure Palladium (.9995 fine)	1 oz. only

Allocated Platinum and Palladium Fund

Recently, the Sprott Asset Management Team started a closed-end trust, which provides a convenient alternative to purchasing and storing physical platinum and palladium. The Sprott Physical Platinum and Palladium Trust (NYSE: SPPP) holds platinum and palladium that is *fully allocated* to investors. This means the bullion is fully tracked. Palladium bullion is stored in secure facilities in London and Zurich and subject to annual external audits to verify amounts held for investors, in addition to frequent inspections. Platinum is stored in a secured facility in Canada. The funds held and invested in the trust are redeemable in the allocated precious metals per Sprott guidelines.

The fund offers similar tax advantages to U.S. investors as the gold (PHYS) and silver (PSLV) funds as long as investors timely file a form 8621 to make a Qualified Electing Fund (QEF) election. The QEF election allows gains realized on sales held for one year or more to be taxed at the long-term capital gains rate (15% for most income earners and 20% for those making over $400,000 single/$450,000 married as of 2013) instead of the collectible rate of 28% applied against precious metal ETF's and coins.

Chapter 17: The Mighty Nickel

How many investments do investors pore over to find one investment with the potential to pay anything close to 30%? What if there is already a guaranteed return on your holdings that exceed even that?

Kyle Bass, a hedge fund manager who made millions betting on the housing crash, purchased over $1,000,000 in nickels. The actual melt value of a nickel, comprised of 25 percent nickel and 75% copper, has a real value of $.068 and rising (subject to change).

Historically, the U.S. government changes the content of coins so they can continue to control and debase fiat currency, and it is likely this will occur with the nickel very soon.

Nickels are already worth 36% more than its stated value subject to fluctuations. This gives nickel owners an automatic 36% return over the face value of the coin.

Savers do not need to convert their retirement accounts into nickels. However, a good strategy is to start making it a habit to periodically exchange your fiat $100 bills for nickels at your bank. What can be a better deal than handing the bank a devaluing Federal Reserve Note in exchange for coins with intrinsic value that is greater than the face amount?

If history is any guide, the Department of the Treasury will not allow coins to circulate that have a value over the nominal (face) value of the coin. Savers simply take them out of circulation and hoard them as their investment increases while the currency is debased. Savers have a small window of time to begin storing nickels that have a value greater than what the U.S. Treasury intended. Take this opportunity to store bags and jars of nickels.

Similar to pre-1965 coins, these coins are easily recognized as U.S. minted coins, and are in small denominations that make them easy to barter. The value of the metals will continue to increase during periods of inflation, and its small denomination makes it a convenient option for trade.

Similarly, the copper in pre-1982 penny is worth 2.39 cents, for an immediate return of 139% to its stated value (subject to change). Unlike the nickel of today, these coins are not widely circulated. In fact, they sell on EBay for three times the face value.

With the nickel, on the other hand, savers still have time to save them now before they are no longer minted.

The U.S. made it illegal to ship these coins totaling over $100 abroad in 2006, but you can store them locally or abroad in safe deposit boxes or depositories.

Chapter 18: Housing in the Fabricated Economy

Housing has continued to stabilize and even recover in many parts of the U.S. With record low mortgage rates and substantially lower housing prices, many investors believe the housing market has finally reached the bottom.

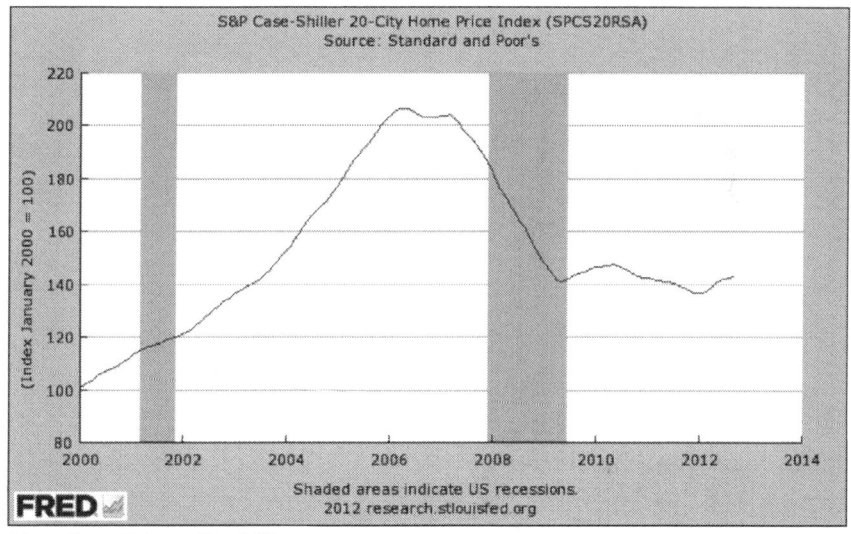

Housing Prices Stabilize

Housing Re-inflated

If the improving housing market was based on rising incomes, lower unemployment, and a real economic recovery based on production, then the housing market would be a good investment opportunity.

Unfortunately the stabilization of the housing market is not based on any of those key factors, but rather on the Federal Reserve lowering interest rates and thereby stabilizing prices with lower mortgage rates. Without this intervention, housing would continue on a downward spiral.

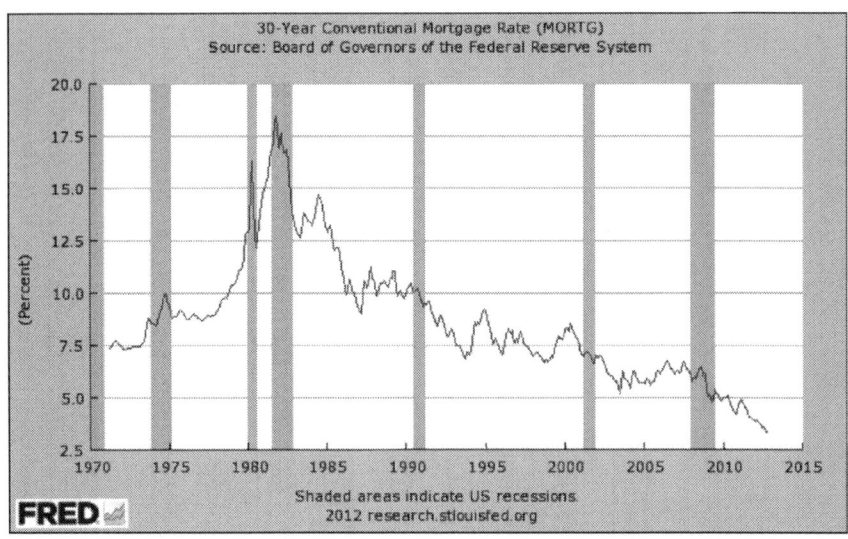

After QE4 the 30-year mortgage reached a record low of close to 3%.

The Federal Reserve has intervened to make up for the fact that real economic drivers of the economy are entirely missing. These missing economic drivers include rising wages, low unemployment, and a productive economy, none of which are present in the current economy.

In fact, real wages have actually dropped to 1969 levels, so housing cannot possibly rise again under these economic downward pressures. With the offshoring of jobs and new college graduates heavily in debt taking lower wage positions, the prospects for the housing market are poor.

Why the Jobs Aren't Coming Back

Additionally, projected job growth over an entire decade for positions requiring a college degree represent only a fraction of the total number of college graduates entering the workforce heavily in debt.

As Dr. Paul Craig Roberts, former Assistant to the Treasury under President Reagan, points out in his book *The Failure of Laissez Faire Capitalism and the Economic Dissolution of the West,* the projected jobs over the entire decade from 2008-2018 requiring a university degree make up only 60% of the number of university graduates in 2012 alone.[56]

Applying this data to 2013, the National Center of Education Statistics projects that 2.6 million students will graduate in the academic year of 2012-2013, including bachelor's degrees, master's degrees, professional degrees, and doctorate degrees.[57] Meanwhile, the Bureau of Labor Statistics projects that jobs requiring a university degree from 2010-2020 will grow by approximately 1.6 million new jobs.[58] This means that new jobs for an entire decade requiring university degrees make up only 62% of the total graduating class of 2013.

Moreover, company executives continue to argue that they are facing a skills gap in the American workforce and must fill many of the remaining jobs left in America with foreign workers. However, due to extensive offshoring of both manufacturing and professional service jobs by companies in America, the truth is that there exists an *oversupply* of skilled workers in America who cannot find jobs. Many of these remaining jobs will be filled by H-1B visa workers as companies continue to spread disinformation in the media and to elected officials that they cannot find skilled workers locally due to a "skills gap" and must expand the H-1B visa program to fill the remaining jobs domestically

This is just another tactic corporations use to lower wages domestically while funneling the increased profits to company

---

[56] (Roberts, The Failure of Laissez Faire Capitalism and the Economic Dissolution of the West, 2013, Kindle Locations 1822-1831)
[57] (Table 247. Earned degrees conferred by degree-granting institutions)
[58] (Table 6: 30 occupations with largest projected employment growth, 2010-20, 2012)

executives. Offshoring and replacing workers domestically are the main reasons why wages and employment have declined in the U.S. while contributing to the widening income gaps in America. The real causes of the labor decline are also why monetary policy has had such a feeble effect on the labor markets: the employment engine that was the basis for a rising middle class has been replaced with globalism under the guise of free trade.

According to many economists, this trend is not reversible since decades of offshoring have already eaten away at the core of America's economy, including all the benefits of manufacturing such as innovation, increased productivity, and invention. All of this was sold for higher profit margins that benefit only a small minority of company executives and stockholders while the middle class continues to vanish.

Low Interest Rates Mask the True Condition of the Housing Market

In late 2008, the Federal Reserve began aggressively lowering the Fed Funds rate to record lows with a commitment to continue the policy well into 2015. The Fed Funds rate is the rate at which banks lend to each other. As the Federal Reserve lowers this primary rate, the cost of credit becomes cheaper for loans across the board, including mortgages. If the rate is raised, on the other hand, banks will pass this cost on to their customers with higher interest rates for various loans.

For example, the 30-year conventional mortgage corresponds to the Fed Funds rate plus approximately 2.82% on average over the past 42 years. This means the Federal Reserve is effectively lowering interest rates, including mortgage rates, to record lows.

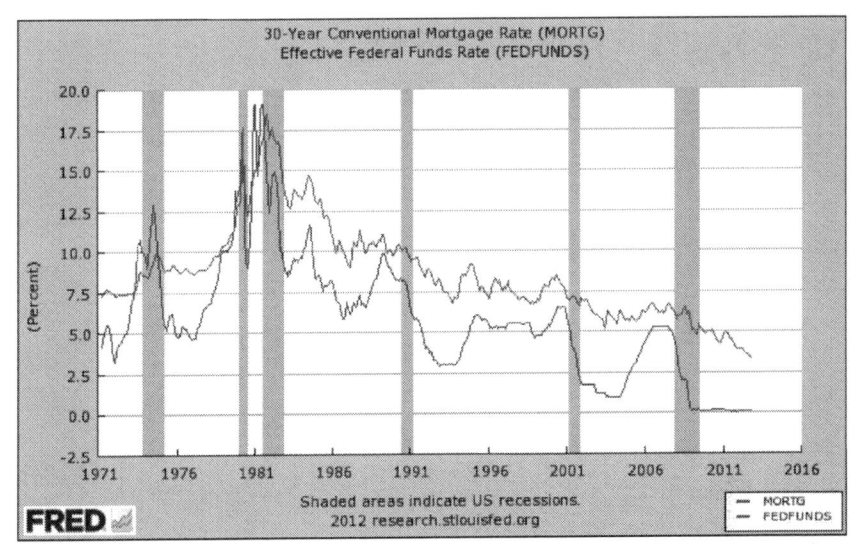

Historically, the 30-year conventional mortgage rate corresponds to the Fed Funds rate plus an average of 2.82% over the past 42 years.

The Federal Reserve has held the Fed Funds rate, the benchmark rate of the Fed, to almost 0% since late 2008, which corresponds to record low mortgage rates.

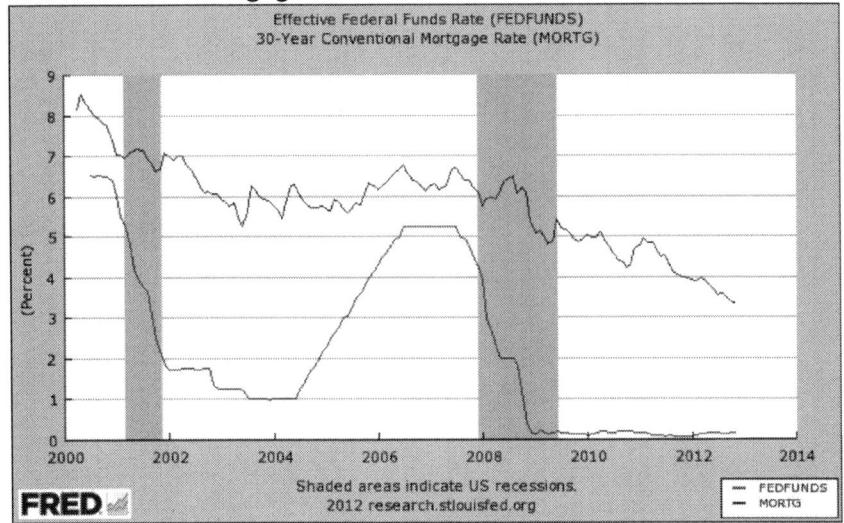

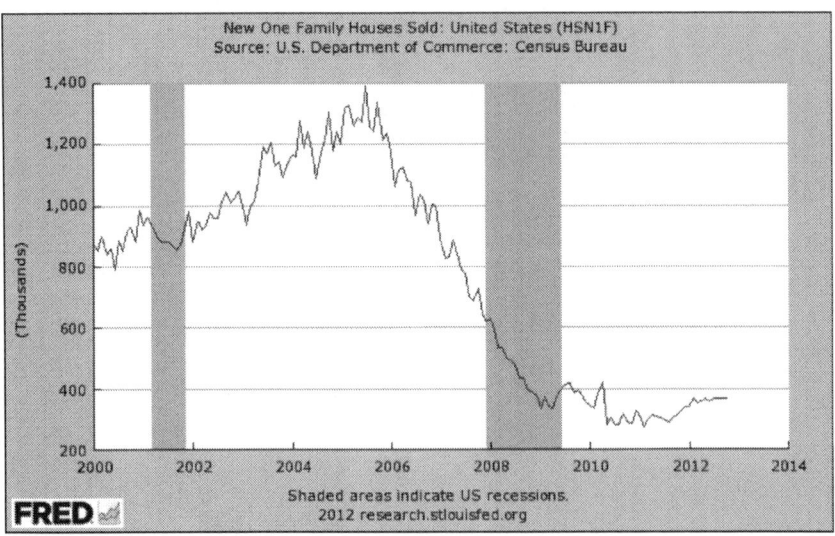

Declining home sales were partially alleviated in 2009, and began to stabilize into 2012 with attractive mortgage rates.

Is this a Good Time to Buy a Home?

With 30-year mortgage rates at record lows of less than 4%, it may be tempting to buy a home. However, rising interest rates have a dramatic impact on real estate prices. As interest rates begin to rise, the value of real estate will drop sharply because the same monthly payment buys less and less real estate.

Rising Mortgage Rates and Home Values

The table and graph below shows how rising interest rates affect real estate prices.

The current 30-year fixed mortgage rate as of the end of the first quarter of 2013 represents the current baseline rate of approximately 3.5%. The horizontal axis and the top portion of the chart represent the rise in interest rates and the bottom half of the chart represents losses in home values. If interest rates rise to just 4%, for example, homeowners face a loss on their home value of almost 6%. A rise in mortgage rates to just 5% represents a loss on home values of more than 16%.

Rising Interest Rates and Home Values

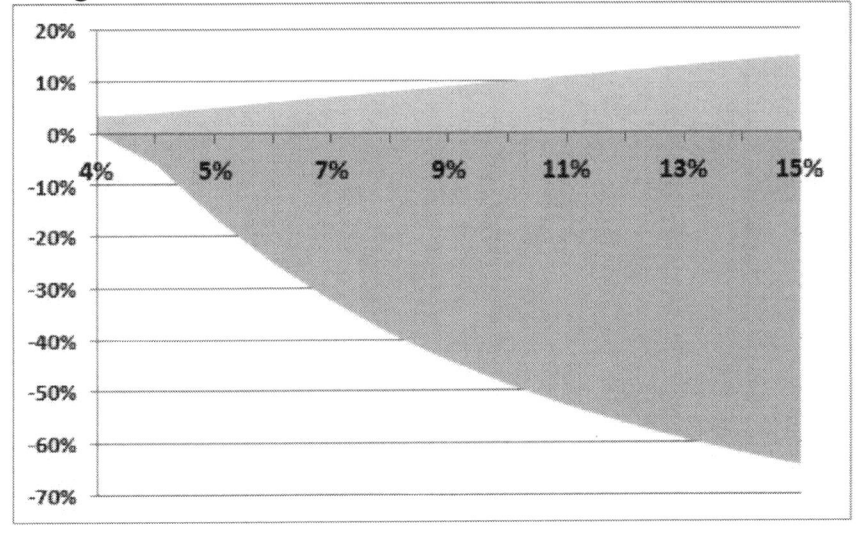

The table below shows rising mortgage rates and losses in home values.

Mortgage Rates	Loss in Home Values
3.50% (Baseline)	0.00%
4.00%	-5.94%
5.00%	-16.35%
6.00%	-25.10%
7.00%	-32.51%
8.00%	-38.80%
9.00%	-44.19%
10.00%	-48.83%
11.00%	-52.85%
12.00%	-56.34%
13.00%	-59.41%
14.00%	-62.10%
15.00%	-64.49%

Homebuyers who plan on staying in the area for a decade or more, and who can get an ultra-low *fixed* rate 30-year mortgage, have a stronger case for buying a home.

When a homebuyer buys a home with little money down and a 30-year mortgage in a pre-inflationary environment, they will pay back the mortgage with devaluing dollars as inflation increases, thereby hedging against inflation. There is no reason to use more valuable dollars now for a large down payment, when a homeowner can pay back the mortgage in devaluing dollars later. Remember that inflation is a debtor's best friend and a creditor's worst enemy.

The one advantage of the housing market now is the low interest rates. Keep in mind that even when a homebuyer buys a home with low interest rates, they still risk losing equity on the home as it decreases in value.

If a homebuyer plans on selling the home within the next few years, then stay out of the housing market altogether.

The Federal Reserve has intervened in the markets to actually recreate the conditions that led to the housing bubble in the first place by purchasing more bonds and mortgage-backed securities (MBS). The Fed's intervention in the bond markets lowers interest rates, and actually encourages banks to continue selling MBS's by purchasing even more of them under QE 3 and QE 4. These conditions wreaked havoc on the housing market and will do so again. Homeowners would not want to *buy and sell a home* in that environment, and similarly would not want to do so now.

Housing Will Continue Its Downward Slide

The real value of homes are likely to decline and in many cases substantially, as many would be buyers are priced out of the market with rising interest rates and rising unemployment.

In nominal terms the price of homes may still increase with inflation, but as the dollar falls and the demand for homes declines with rising interest rates, the price of homes in *real terms* will also fall.

That is why it is important that homebuyers do not plan on selling their home for many years if they buy a home during this reprieve in the housing market's downward slide.

In the aftermath of the financial collapse, which will include the collapse of the bond market, the dollar, and housing, investors who hedged against inflation with the strategies outlined in this book will be able to pick up homes for pennies on the dollar. When investors cash in gold for other hard assets, for example, they will have lost nothing to inflation and will be able to use the preserved capital to pick up a homes and properties when prices truly reach the bottom.

Until that time, potential homebuyers should only consider buying a home for a ***primary residence*** if they plan on living there long-term, and are able to get an ultra-low ***fixed*** rate 30-year mortgage. Homeowners who have low interest rates and a fixed rate mortgage are eliminating a substantial expense from the budget, locking in a reasonable housing payment over the long-term, and paying back the mortgage with devaluing dollars.

If you plan on selling your home within the next few years, sell sooner rather than later. As home prices decline, more and more buyers will realize that the housing recovery was only temporary.

Investment Properties

Most investment properties are not a good buy under any scenario even with low interest rates, because the other economic fundamentals to support housing prices are missing entirely.

Housing is a function of leverage even when homeowners pay cash, and rising interest rates will reduce demand for homes. Though more people not able to afford homes will rent, rising unemployment will leave many rentals vulnerable to losses in both equity through rising interest rates and income through rising unemployment.

Any stability in the housing market is based on the Federal Reserve keeping interest rates artificially low. Homeowners should use this temporary reprieve to sell investment properties, vacation homes, and other real estate. The housing recovery and low interest rates are an economic fabrication that is not based ample savings and demand, high employment, and rising wages. It is another bubble that will pop similar to the financial crisis of 2008 except worse.

Better Options

The best option is to place more of your assets in inflation protected assets like gold, and then pick up a home for pennies on the dollar in the aftermath of the financial collapse. In many cases homebuyers won't even need a mortgage, because prices will be so low that they can purchase the home at rock bottom prices when the housing market runs its course and finally hits bottom. The Federal Reserve may have halted the housing decline, but it is only temporary and will make the situation much worse in the long-term.

Chapter 19: Peer Lending

In a world of suppressed interest rates, investors are finding it harder and harder to find investments that offer them a reasonable return on their money.

Peer lending has emerged as a new vehicle that allows investors to earn a higher return without resorting to risky investments like junk bonds. Peer lending also brings the investor and borrower together directly while eliminating big banks that often charge big fees. The peer lending platform empowers investors to directly screen for risk and reward and lend directly to borrowers.

Lending Club

The Lending Club arrived on the scene in 2007 to fill this demand for higher yields outside the control of central banking.

Lending Club has funded over $1.1 billion in loans, and paid over $100 million in interest to investors since inception. It focuses mainly on low-risk borrowers with an average FICO score of 715.

The Lending Club approves fewer than 10% of loan applicants to start with before the investor even begins the screening process.

The Lending Club's peer lending technology then allows investors to directly screen for risk/reward factors for each loan they wish to fund. The risk category runs from grades A1, which is the highest quality investment, to grade G5, which is the riskiest investment. The higher the risk of each loan, the higher the interest rate. For example, Grade A loans average 7.51% returns as of December 2012, and Grade G loans average 22.51%.

Investors can then screen for loan details such as rate, loan terms, FICO score, amount, and the percent currently funded with amount/time left.

From there investors can dig even deeper with 23 additional filters such as "Max Debt-to-Income Ratio", "Loan Purpose," "Verified Income," "Min Length of Employment," and "Home Ownership." Investors can spread the risk across different loans, and invest as little as $25 for each loan, or fund the entire balance of the loan.

Lending Club recommends spreading your money across many notes, as those investors with 800 notes or more have experienced 100% positive returns with 93.65% of them earning 6% to 18% on their investments. For example, if you have $5,000 to invest, Lending Club recommends spreading $25 across 200 notes each instead of investing the entire $5,000 in one note. If one borrower becomes delinquent, it represents only .5% of your investment across 200 notes instead of 100% of your investment at risk when you invest in only one borrower.

The notes generate monthly cash flow to the investor, while Lending Club handles all of the loan processing details such as interest charges, late fees, service fees, loan approvals, etc. In return, Lending Club charges investors 1% on amounts paid from borrowers for servicing the loans.

Investors can even open a Traditional IRA, Roth IRA, and other retirement accounts to invest in. This also creates a tax efficient way of tracking your earnings.

The notes can be sold on the secondary market before maturity through its secondary market platform in partnership with Folio Investing. Folio charges the seller a 1% trading fee on each note sold.

Recently Larry Summers and John Mack joined the board of directors. John Mack served as CEO of Morgan Stanley from June 2005 – December of 2009 when the company was overwhelmed with toxic assets and required billions in government aid to stay afloat. Larry Summers served as Treasury Secretary under Bill Clinton where he oversaw the deregulation of the financial sector that led to the financial crisis of 2008. Let's hope that Lending Club stays on track with bringing the borrower and lender together by offering quality risk analysis with low fees.

Prosper

Prosper was launched in 2006 as the first peer-to-peer lending company. It has over 1.5 million members and over $441 million in funded loans as of December 2012. Prosper also offers peer lending to investors with notes starting as low as $25 so investors can diversify their holdings across many loans.

Investments are categorized from lower risk returns with AA ratings to investments with the highest risk and yield rated HR. AA investments average a returns of 5.21%, and investments in the HR category earn average returns of 14.12%. The total average return across all investments is 9.69% as of September 2012.

Prosper allows investors to filter for specific loans that meet their criteria such as loan type, loan terms, employment requirements, etc. Prosper focuses creditworthy borrowers and accepts only 10% of loan applicants before investors even begin to filter through the loans.

The notes generate monthly cash flow to the investor less a 1% servicing fee. Moreover, the notes can be sold on the secondary market before maturity through its secondary market platform in partnership with Folio Investing. Folio Investing charges a 1% fee on the face amount of each note sold.

In the U.K., similar peer-to-peer lending services are Zopa and Funding Circle.

Conclusion

The financial crisis that Americans experienced in 2008 was the prelude to a much greater financial storm brewing over the U.S. economy right now with gathering force. Those who are not prepared stand to lose trillions in savings, pension funds, and retirement accounts.

Our economy over the past few decades was built on the illusion that credit and consumption could somehow replace production because the U.S. was able to fund its deficits with the world reserve currency and growing debt. This caused the United States to transition from the world's largest creditor nation to the world's largest debtor nation. In the latter decades wealth was further leeched out of the economy with toxic derivatives, fraud, and market manipulations that were added to an already toxic mix of excessive credit.

There is no historical precedent for nations running debts of over $60 trillion, derivatives markets of over $800 trillion, and the heedless expansion of credit based on a fractional amount of assets. This is why gold, a real asset selected by the market as a store of value for thousands of years, will return as a safe haven as the rush away from credit and fiat currencies escalates. Many investors will begin to realize that gold is immune to inflation, interest rate manipulation, and central planning mismanagement, and will rush to this proven store of value during financial upheaval and collapse.

Though gold may enter its own bubble for which investors stand to make tremendous returns, the main objective is for investors to position their assets, savings, and wealth out of the way of the storm's path, so that when the financial system collapses, those prepared do not go down with it. Those who are prepared for the coming disruptions in the financial markets will be in a position to reestablish themselves financially and to help rebuild.

This begins by diversifying out of dollar based assets into hard assets. Only hard assets will survive a paper collapse. Additionally, prepared investors will be able to use ongoing market manipulations in their favor to purchase real assets at a discount before they skyrocket in value. As investors position their assets to safely ride out the financial collapse, they can also quickly reestablish themselves in a post-collapse economy.

The Federal Reserve cannot hold interest rates down forever, and when rates begin to slowly rise, this should be a clear warning sign that inflation and financial instability are on the horizon. This financial crisis will unfortunately be far worse than the 2008 crisis since not only were the same problems not corrected, but they were compounded with low interest rates and cheap money fed to the same financial institutions that caused the crisis.

Politicians will continue to debate and dismiss sensitive topics like gold and the dollar's diminishing status worldwide while the price of gold and other precious metals continues to rise long-term while experiencing short-term volatility. Additionally, central banks dismissing gold as money will actively acquire it and even repatriate gold not held in their possession for decades as we are already witnessing.

Investors well prepared will have the added benefit of riding the bubbles that ensue afterward, like precious metals. Precious metals are not immune from bubbles, and when panicked investors and banks head to this asset as a last resort while the bond markets and dollar collapse, early precious metal buyers will already have invested early enough to ride it to the top. When housing, land, stocks, and other assets truly reach the bottom, investors who properly guarded against inflation will have the savings and wealth to buy these assets for a fraction of the pre-collapse era cost.

This book is designed to prepare you for the worst so you can come to the other side better off and better prepared to rebuild a productive economy after the unprecedented financial collapse ahead.

Bibliography

Meet the Press Transcript for August 7, 2011. (2011, August 7). Retrieved from Meet the Press Transcript for August 7, 2011: http://www.msnbc.msn.com/id/44050464/ns/meet_the_press-transcripts/t/meet-press-transcript-august/

Reserve Requirements. (2011, October 26). Retrieved from Federal Reserve: http://www.federalreserve.gov/monetarypolicy/reservereq.htm

Chairman Bernanke's Press Conference. (2012, September 13). Retrieved from Board of Governors of the Federal Reserve System: http://federalreserve.gov/

China and Brazil in $30bn Currency Swap Agreement. (2012, June 22). Retrieved from BBC News: http://www.bbc.co.uk/news/business-18545978

China Buying Oil from Iran with Yuan. (2012, May 8). Retrieved from BBC News: http://www.bbc.co.uk/news/business-17988142

China, Germany Plan to Settle More Trade in Yuan, Euros. (2012, August 30). Retrieved from Reuters: http://www.reuters.com/article/2012/08/30/germany-china-yuan-idUSB4E7JG00D20120830

Table 6: 30 occupations with largest projected employment growth, 2010-20. (2012, February 1). Retrieved from Bureau of Labor Statistics: http://www.bls.gov/news.release/ecopro.t06.htm

Factors Affecting Reserve Balances of Depository Institutions and Condition Statement of Federal Reserve Banks. (2013, April 18). Retrieved from Federal Reserve: http://www.federalreserve.gov/releases/h41/current/

Government - Interest Expense on the Outstanding Debt. (2013, June 6). Retrieved from Treasury Direct: http://www.treasurydirect.gov/govt/reports/ir/ir_expense.htm

U.S. International Reserve Position. (2013, April 12). Retrieved from U.S. Department of the Treasury: http://www.treasury.gov/resource-center/data-chart-center/IR-Position/Pages/04122013.aspx

Appelbaum, B. (2012, February 27). *A U.S. Boon in Low-Cost Borrowing*. Retrieved from The New York Times: http://www.nytimes.com/2012/02/28/business/era-of-low-cost-borrowing-benefits-federal-government.html?_r=0

Bloomberg. (2012, June 19). *Jamie Dimon, Welfare Recepient*. Retrieved from www.money.msn.com: http://money.msn.com/investing/jamie-dimon-welfare-recipient-bloomberg.aspx

Callick, R. (2013, March 30). *PM Set to Sign China Currency Deal in Boost to Exporters*. Retrieved from The Australian: http://www.theaustralian.com.au/national-affairs/foreign-affairs/pm-set-to-sign-china-currency-deal-in-boost-to-exporters/story-fn59nm2j-1226609244139

Cauchon, D. (2011, June 13). *U.S. Funding for Future Promises Lags by Trillions*. Retrieved from USA Today: http://www.usatoday.com/news/washington/2011-06-06-us-owes-62-trillion-in-debt_n.htm

CFTC. (2010, March 25). *Public Meeting to Examine Futures and Options Trading in the Metals Markets.* Retrieved from CFTC: http://www.cftc.gov/

Corkery, S. N. (2012, August 21). *Buffet's Muni-Bond Move Raises a Red Flag*. Retrieved from The Wall Street Journal Online: www.online.wsj.com

Cox, C., & Archer, B. (2012, November 26). *Cox and Archer: Why $16 Trillion Only Hints at the True U.S. Debt*. Retrieved from The Wall Street Journal: http://online.wsj.com/article/SB10001424127887323353204578127374039087636.html

Erste, G. R. (2010, June 21). *Gold Report 2010 - In Gold We Trust*. Retrieved from www.erstegroup.com: www.erstegroup.com

Erste, G. R. (2012, July 11). *Gold Report 2012 - In Gold We Trust*. Retrieved from www.erstegroup.com: www.erstegroup.com/de/Downloads/0901481b800bb26c.pdf

FDIC. (2013, March 28). *http://www.fdic.gov/deposit/insurance/fund.html*. Retrieved from http://www.fdic.gov/: http://www.fdic.gov/deposit/insurance/memo_2013_03_28.pdf

Federal Reserve Bank. (2012, 10 1). *FRED Economic Data*. Retrieved from National Composite Home Price Index for the United States: http://research.stlouisfed.org/datatools.html

Federal Reserve Bank. (2013, March 1). *FRED Economic Data*. Retrieved from Effective Federal Funds Rate, Monthly, Not Seasonally Adjusted: http://research.stlouisfed.org/

Fontevecchia, A. (2011, November 15). *Is GLD Really as Good as Gold?* Retrieved from Forbes: http://www.forbes.com/sites/afontevecchia/2011/11/15/is-gld-really-as-good-as-gold/

Guilyeva, H. (2012, July 9). *What's Iran Doing with Turkish Gold?* Retrieved from ft.com: http://blogs.ft.com/beyond-brics/2012/07/09/whats-iran-doing-with-all-that-turkish-gold/#axzz22QUWaA3w

Hall, C. (2012, January 18). *China Signs Currency Swap Deal with UAE*. Retrieved from Financial Times: http://www.ft.com/cms/s/0/82e5d5b8-41da-11e1-a586-00144feab49a.html#axzz29OesA9oX

Ivry, B., Son, H., & Harper, C. (2011, October 18). *BofA Said to Split Regulators Over Moving Merrill Derivatives to Bank Unit*. Retrieved from Bloomberg: http://www.bloomberg.com/news/2011-10-18/bofa-said-to-split-regulators-over-moving-merrill-derivatives-to-bank-unit.html

Kessler, A. S. (2012, October). *The Renminbi Bloc Is Here: Asia Down, Rest of the World to Go?* Retrieved from Peterson

King, E. (2013, April 16). *Bullion Shortages Develop As Retail Demand Skyrockets*. Retrieved from KingWorldNews: http://kingworldnews.com/kingworldnews/KWN_DailyWeb/Entries/2013/4/16_Bullion_Shortages_Develop_As_Retail_Demand_Skyrockets.html

Institute for International Economics: http://www.iie.com/publications/interstitial.cfm?ResearchID=2241

Mukherji, B., & Nayak, D. (2013, April 23). *India Gold Premiums Soar as Demand Outstrips Supply*. Retrieved from The Wall Street Journal: http://online.wsj.com/article/SB10001424127887324874204578440242906344734.html

Norman, R. (2013, April 15). *Gold Crushed by 400 Tonnes or $20 Billion of Selling on COMEX*. Retrieved from SharpsPixley: http://news.sharpspixley.com/article/ross-norman-gold-crushed-by-400-tonnes-or-usd20-billion-of-selling-on-comex/159239/

OCC. (1998, December 31). *OCC Bank Derivatives Report Fourth Quarter 1998*. Retrieved from Office of the Comptroller of the Currency, U.S. Department of the Treasury: http://www.occ.gov/topics/capital-markets/financial-markets/trading/derivatives/dq498.pdf

OCC. (2008, December 31). *OCC's Quarterly Report on Bank Trading and Derivatives Activities Fourth Quarter 2008*. Retrieved from Office of the Comptroller of the Currency; U.S. Department of the Treasury: http://www.occ.gov/topics/capital-markets/financial-markets/trading/derivatives/dq408.pdf

OCC. (2012, December 31). *OCC's Quarterly Report on Bank Trading and Derivatives Activities Fourth Quarter 2012*. Retrieved from Office of the Comptroller of the Currency; U.S. Department of the Treasury: http://www.occ.treas.gov/topics/capital-markets/financial-markets/trading/derivatives/dq412.pdf

Pilar, R. ". (2011, October 4). *U.S.- China-Japan Relations, U.S. Policy, China's Gold Reserves*. Retrieved from www.wikileaks.org: http://wikileaks.org/cable/2009/04/09BEIJING1134.html

PressTV.ir. (2012, February 28). *Iran to Ditch Dollar in Foreign Trades: CBI Governor*. Retrieved from PressTV.ir: http://www.presstv.ir/detail/229045.html

Pritchard, A. E. (2013, January 15). *Bundesbank to Pull Gold from New York and Paris in Watershed Moment*. Retrieved from The Telegraph: http://www.telegraph.co.uk/finance/personalfinance/investing/gold/9804444/Bundesbank-to-pull-gold-from-New-York-and-Paris-in-watershed-moment.html

Qingfen, L. X. (2012, July 4). *Japan 'Must End Outdated Policy'*. Retrieved from ChinaDaily.com: http://www.chinadaily.com.cn/china/2012-07/04/content_15546502.htm

Research, E. G. (2010, June 21). *Gold Report 2010 - In Gold We Trust*. Retrieved from www.erstegroup.com: www.erstegroup.com

Research, E. G. (2012, July 11). *Gold Report 2012 - In Gold We Trust*. Retrieved from www.erstegroup.com: www.erstegroup.com/de/Downloads/0901481b800bb26c.pdf

Roberts, D. P. (2013, April 13). *Assault on Gold Update*. Retrieved from Paul Craig Roberts: http://www.paulcraigroberts.org/2013/04/13/assault-on-gold-update-paul-craig-roberts/

Roberts, D. P. (2013). *The Failure of Laissez Faire Capitalism and the Economic Dissolution of the West*. Kindle Edition: Atwell Publishing.

RT.com. (2012, March 20). *BRICS Bank Next Step to Dollar Independence*. Retrieved from RT.com: http://rt.com/business/news/brics-set-bank-development-004/

Schweitzer, M. a. (2009, January 21). *Federal Reserve Bank of Cleveland*. Retrieved from Adjustable-Rate Mortgages and the Libor Surprise: http://www.clevelandfed.org/research/commentary/2009/012109.cfm

Schweizer, P. (2012, February 9). *Warren Buffet: Baptist and Bootlegger*. Retrieved from Reason.com: http://reason.com/archives/2012/02/09/warren-buffett-baptist-and-bootlegger

Scott, R. E. (2011, September 20). *Growing U.S. Trade Deficit with China Cost 2.8 Million Jobs Between 2001 and 2010*. Retrieved from www.epi.org: http://www.epi.org/publication/growing-trade-deficit-china-cost-2-8-million/

Siegel, J. J. (2005). *The Future for Investors.* New York: Crown Publishing Group.

Skeel, D. (2010). *The New Financial Deal: Understanding the Dodd-Frank Act and Its (Unintended) Consequences.* John Wiley and Sons.

Table 247. Earned degrees conferred by degree-granting institutions. (n.d.). Retrieved from National Center for Education Statistics: http://nces.ed.gov/programs/digest/d04/tables/dt04_247.asp

Thurber, J. (2012, April 17). *Edward Humes Enjoys Digging Through Rubbish*. Retrieved from Los Angeles Times: http://articles.latimes.com/2012/apr/17/entertainment/la-et-0417-edward-humes-20120417

Toscano, B. (2012, February 3). *Biggest Holders of US Government Debt*. Retrieved from CNBC: http://www.cnbc.com/id/29880401/The_Biggest_Holders_of_US_Government_Debt

White, G. (2012, August 19). *Are We About to See A Chinese Gold Rush?* Retrieved from The Telegraph: http://www.telegraph.co.uk/finance/personalfinance/inve

sting/gold/9486294/Are-we-about-to-see-a-Chinese-gold-rush.html

Xiaokun, S. Q. (2010, November 24). *China, Russia Quit Dollar*. Retrieved from ChinaDaily.com: http://www.chinadaily.com.cn/china/2010-11/24/content_11599087.htm

Made in the USA
Middletown, DE
07 November 2016